Praise for Christine Foster Meloni's
Growing Up in Mussolini's Fascist Italy

"At the crossroads of biography, memoir, essay, and history, *Growing Up in Mussolini's Fascist Italy: The Story of Andrea Marcello Meloni* is a vivid and moving tribute to a unique period in time and a unique individual who lived through it. Weaving firsthand accounts and photographs with a wealth of research and insights, Christine Foster Meloni gives us a detailed excavation of a period that is no less fascinating or relevant now than it was when it occurred, and she paints a memorable portrait of a man who was forever altered by it.
- Kirk Kjeldsen, author of *Land of Hidden Fires*

"Often left out of World War II accounts set in Europe, *Growing Up in Mussolini's Fascist Italy: The Story of Andrea Marcello Meloni* offers a vivid picture of life in Italy during Mussolini's 21-year iron rule. "When I was born, in 1928," Andrea writes, "I was born a little fascist. Yes! In that period one was first born a fascist and then an Italian." In this memoir, author Christine Meloni wraps her husband's own words in her own extensive research on the rise of Mussolini and the historical context of Andrea's life. This is both an entertaining and informative read for anyone interested in World War II history and fascism in Italy."
-J.L. Oakley, author of *The Jøssing Affair* and *The Quisling Factor*

**Also by
Christine Foster Meloni**

Say the Right Thing: A Functional Approach to Developing Speaking Skills

Internet for English Teaching (with Mark Warschauer and Heidi Shetzer)

Powdered Peas and Other Blessings: Life in an Orphanage in Naples, Italy

Il Miracolo dei Santi: 100 Anni di Casa Materna

Growing Up in Mussolini's Fascist Italy

The Story of Andrea Marcello Meloni

Christine Foster Meloni

Copyright © 2020 by Christine Foster Meloni.

ISBN: Softcover   978-1-7960-7475-8
          eBook   978-1-7960-7474-1

All rights reserved. No part of this book may be reproduced or transmitted in any form or by any means, electronic or mechanical, including photocopying, recording, or by any information storage and retrieval system, without permission in writing from the copyright owner.

Any people depicted in stock imagery provided by Getty Images are models, and such images are being used for illustrative purposes only.
Certain stock imagery © Getty Images.

Print information available on the last page.

Cover Photograph by Nicola Morano

Rev. date: 07/16/2020

To order additional copies of this book, contact:
Xlibris
1-888-795-4274
www.Xlibris.com
Orders@Xlibris.com
781335

To Our Grandchildren
Claudia, Christian, Paul, Colin, and Arthur
and
To Our Godchildren
Perry and Chipo
Who all loved Andrea and will keep his memory alive

In Loving Memory of
Gabriella Testa Cahill
(1922-2020)

Acknowledgments

I have many special friends and family to thank for their assistance with this book. I am very grateful for the love that all of them have shown me, knowing that Andrea's words were so very dear to my heart and that, with this book, I hope to keep his memory alive.

To my many friends in the Washburn High School Class of 1959 whose enthusiastic reception to my Lyceum talk on Andrea's memoir at our 60th Class Reunion inspired me to write this book

To Indra Corea, Marie Hansen, Ivan Olesov, Larisa Olesova, John Olsen, Janet Quinn, and John Quinn who participated in a focus group to give me advice on my preliminary ideas for the book

To Robin Alexander, Roger Anderson, William Apple, Susan Bayley, George Bozzini, Tim Christenson, Barbara Christy, Indra Corea, Stephen Elliott, William Greer, Marie Hansen, Elizabeth Hardisty, John Paul Kennedy, Nicoletta Meloni, Barbara Myklebust, Janet Oakley, Kim O'Connell, Terry Parssinen, Janet Quinn, and Kate Vellenich who were my dedicated readers and gave me valuable feedback on my manuscript

To my niece Silvia Meloni, a current resident of Acuto, who provided me with significant historical information about the German occupation of Acuto and its liberation by the Allies

To Gabriella Testa Cahill who shared personal stories of surviving the Allied bombing of her hometown of Livorno

To Sergio D'Onofrio who shared personal stories of his family's suffering when the 71st Division of the German army set up its command center in their town of Coreno near Cassino, where one of the bloodiest battles of WWII took place, the Battle of Montecassino

To Fred Berg and Del Syverson who shared their personal stories of serving in the U.S. Army in WWII in Italy and to their wives Ginnie Berg and Dolores Syverson and Del's son Johnne Syverson for providing documents, diaries, and photographs

To Betsy Mignani who provided photographs and drawings

To Bruno Diconi, Marisa Diconi, and Carlo Mignani who grew up in Italy and gave me an important Italian perspective

To Kristina Anderson, Linda Sponsler, and Dona De Sanctis who offered encouraging support and constructive suggestions

I ask for the forgiveness of those I may have inadvertently omitted.

Contents

Dedication v
Acknowledgments vii
Preface xi
Readers, Please Take Note xiii

Chapter 1   The Fascist Education of Andrea Meloni 1
Chapter 2   The Pact of Steel Between Mussolini and
               Hitler: 1940-1943 26
Chapter 3   Civil War in Italy and The Nazi Occupation of
               Rome: July 1943 – June 1944 35
Chapter 4   The Liberation of Rome in June 1944 and
               Continued Challenges 51
Chapter 5   Lasting Effects on Andrea of Living Under Fascism 59
Chapter 6   Andrea's Postwar Life in Italy and The United States ... 69

Author's Notes 73
References 87

Preface

When my husband Andrea Meloni was born, in 1928, Benito Mussolini was in power at the head of Italy's fascist government. Living the first 18 years of his life under this autocratic regime had a profound effect on Andrea, in particular on his way of thinking and his way of seeing the world.

As an adult, he became a serious World War II buff, reading everything about the war that he could get his hands on. He also enjoyed sharing his own memories with his family and friends, who strongly encouraged him to write them down. He finally picked up a pencil and a yellow legal pad and began to write.

When he finished, I made copies for his family in Italy. I then translated his text into English and gave copies to his relatives in the United States. Everyone found it very interesting reading and a valuable record of their personal family history.

We all thought, however, that his story had universal appeal. Many people are interested in World War II as evidenced by the large number of books published on the subject every year. Andrea left an important personal account of what it was like to be a child and then a teenager in those years. He tells how happy he was to be a little soldier with his friends, marching through the streets of Rome and catching frequent glimpses of Mussolini. At a certain point, his outlook changed. He was no longer keen to find himself in a fascist regime with its restrictions and with the suffering caused by Italy's participation in World War II.

I decided, therefore, to prepare his manuscript for publication. I felt that additional historical context was needed, and so I began to research the subject. I was overwhelmed by the vast amount of material and tried to narrow down what I read to material directly relevant to Andrea's personal account.

This book is my memorial to my beloved husband, the very special Roman with whom I spent fifty extraordinary years. Preparing it has been a true labor of love. I hope he would be pleased.

Christine Foster Meloni
Washington, DC
2020

Readers, Please Take Note

1. Quotations from Andrea's memoir

Throughout the book, in order to make Andrea's own words stand out, the longer excerpts taken from his memoir appear in paragraph form and are written in italics and enclosed within quotation marks.

Here is an example:

"The Mace Bearer carried a baton with a silver knob at the top and an ornamental ribbon and marched ahead of everyone, in the middle of the street, and provided the tempo for the march, by making his baton spin with great mastery and musical ability."

2. Translated material

Quotations from sources originally written in Italian or French were translated by the author unless otherwise noted.

Chapter One

The Fascist Education of Andrea Meloni

BACKGROUND: MUSSOLINI'S RISE TO POWER

Benito Mussolini established the National Fascist Party in Italy on November 7, 1921. He came to power the following year when he was appointed Prime Minister by Victor Emmanuel III, King of Italy.

Victor Emmanuel III

Before becoming a fascist, however, Mussolini had been active in Italy's Socialist Party. His father was a socialist and named him Benito after the leftist president of Mexico, Benito Juárez. His middle names, Amilcare and Andrea, came from two Italian socialists, Amilcare Cipriani and Andrea Costa.

While living in Switzerland from 1902 to 1904, he became a journalist and wrote for periodicals such as *L'Avvenire del Lavoratore* (The Future of the Worker). In 1912, he became editor of *Avanti!* (Forward!), the official daily newspaper of Italy's Socialist Party. He preached revolution and class conflict and spoke out against patriotism. He supported the fundamental tenet of the party: Italy's neutrality in World War I.

Mussolini's position on the war suddenly changed radically, however, and he came to favor intervention. For this stand he was expelled from the Party. He served in the war until he was wounded and discharged in 1917. He then began to preach nationalism instead of socialism.

After the war, there was considerable unrest in Italy because many Italians were displeased with its meager gains. At the signing of the Treaty of Versailles, Great Britain and France reneged on their promise to grant Italy certain territorial gains on the eastern coast of the Adriatic Sea and in Africa.

In her paper, "The Road to Fascism: Mussolini's Transition from Socialism to Nationalism," Kelly Oeltjenbruns (2015) states

> Mussolini's shift is undeniable and significant; such a substantial ideological shift from (refined) Marxist-socialism to Italian fascism and nationalism is indeed the subject of much debate among scholars.

She presents the conflicting theories of three scholars. Zeev Sternhell suggests that the pragmatism of Mussolini was the primary force for his shift while Peter Neville attributes it to his aggressive and inconsistent personality, as already evidenced in his childhood. Anthony Gregor, on the other hand, believes that Mussolini had a sincere Nationalist change of heart. Oeltjenbruns herself favors Sternhell's theory[1].

---

[1] Sternhell is considered one of the leading experts on fascism.

Historian Terry Parssinen points out that, after the end of WWI, in 1918, many Europeans struggled to align themselves with the ideology that would best help their country recover from the war. He believes that Mussolini realized that Italy's disappointment in not being amply rewarded at the Paris Peace Conference provided the boost for a nationalist political stance that would be more likely to bring him to power, which it did. He mentions that it is not often known that Hitler also briefly aligned with socialism before finding his "true calling" in the Nazi Party. (Email message to author, January 27, 2020)

Mussolini took advantage of the precarious post-war situation in Italy and organized the March on Rome with his Black Shirts (mostly discontented WWI soldiers) with the goal of overtaking the government. According to British journalist David Willey (2002), there was no march. Mussolini created the myth that he and an army of 300,000 fascists had marched on Rome on October 28, 1922. In truth, they had travelled to Rome from Milan by train in first class and the number of Black Shirts was probably closer to a few hundred.

This march, however, convinced the King, who was eager to end the unrest, that Mussolini might be just the person to bring order and stability to the country. So he appointed him Prime Minister on October 31, 1922. That year signaled the beginning of the fascist era and became *Year I* of the fascist calendar.

Benito Mussolini

What exactly is fascism? The word comes from *fasci*, an Italian term for "a bundle of sticks" that symbolizes strength in unity. Fascists believed that, if Italians were united under one leader, Italy would become a more powerful nation.

The Cambridge Online Dictionary defines fascism as "*A political system based on a very powerful leader, state control of social and economic life, and extreme pride in country and race, with no expression of political disagreement allowed.*"

This definition would certainly apply to the regime of Mussolini, which lasted from 1922 to 1943. According to the celebrated Italian intellectual, Umberto Eco,

> Italian fascism was the first right-wing dictatorship that took over a European country, and all similar movements later found a sort of archetype in Mussolini's regime. Italian fascism was the first to establish a military liturgy, a folklore, even a way of dressing – far more influential, with its black shirts, than Armani, Benetton, or Versace would ever be. (Eco 1995)

Andrea's Early Childhood in Acuto

"When I was born, in 1928, I was born a little fascist. Yes! In that period one was first born a fascist and then an Italian."

Andrea was born in Anno VI (Year Six) of the Fascist Era. His birthplace was Acuto, a small village located on a ridge in the Monti Ernici mountain range in central Italy, about 60 kilometers (37 miles) east of Rome. Poverty was widespread and his family too was very poor.

View of Acuto
Photograph by the author

"With the exception of a quarry which extracted lime from the mountain's limestone and gave work to just a few people, who were lucky to have a job but unlucky to have to breathe the dust, there were no other ways of earning money in Acuto. A great part of the population, men as well as women, in order to earn a little money, were forced to leave the village and go to Rome or to a nearby village which offered better working opportunities."

"My father Antonio occasionally went to work in Rome for the Puricelli Company, which had a contract with the city council to pave the streets with both asphalt and 'sanpietrini' (a kind of cobblestone). When not working in Rome, my father had a sharecropping contract with the family of Peppino Pompili for the farming of some land. Thus, our household was provided with wheat and corn."

"During the olive-picking season he worked as a day laborer, and sometimes my mother Assunta went to work with him. For every day they worked, they earned a certain amount of olive oil but no cash. In our house there was always a large chest made of dark wood with a cover and legs to keep flour and bread and a terracotta *container with a wooden lid that held about 50 or 100 liters of olive oil."*

"My mother Assunta also went to work a couple of times a year in the vineyards, both those close to Acuto and others near Rome in the Castelli Romani (the Roman hill towns), to weed the vineyards, to remove superfluous leaves from vines so that the little grape stalks could get enough sun, and to pick grapes."

Their "house" in Acuto was built against the side of a rock. It consisted of only one room that served as a living room, dining room, and bedroom for two adults and three children. There was no kitchen and no bathroom.

Andrea at age two in Acuto
Photograph by Nicola Morano

"At this time there was no running water in the houses. It was necessary to go to the public fountain for water. This was the responsibility of the women. The container they used was a 'conca.' The conca held ten or fifteen liters and was made of copper. The village women, once they had filled the conca with water, put it

on their hip or balanced it on their heads, and carried it home. To wash our clothing, my mother would go with the other women to the communal laundry outside of the village."

As an adult, Andrea bought the miniature conca shown in the photo below to remind him of his mother and his early years in Acuto.

A Conca
Photograph by the author

"Since there was no plumbing in the houses, there were no toilets. We had to go outside. We went into the stable that was a few steps from our house. There was usually a donkey in the stable and so all of our excrements and those of the donkey were collected and mixed with hay and straw and, every now and then, they were carried in an appropriate container out into the fields and used as fertilizer."

"There was no electricity. I remember my mother returning from the forest with a bundle of wood on her head. Burning wood in the fireplace was the only way to cook because liquid gas and natural gas were not yet available in Acuto. It was also the only way to keep warm. To make bread, she prepared the loaves of dough at home and then carried them to the communal oven."

"In order to save on the consumption of wood and matches, we children were given a tin can with holes in the bottom and on the sides, suspended with an iron wire of about half a meter in length, and we went to our neighbors who already had a lit fire. We put a few

of their coals in the can which we rolled all the way home so that air would go through the holes to provide oxygen to keep the coals lit."

"We all slept in one bed on a sack stuffed with corn husks that had been dried and then chopped up to make them softer before inserting them into the sack. As these husks flattened out with use, every once in a while the sack had to be reopened to insert more husks in order to raise its level. Not only was the mattress uncomfortable, it was also noisy. Whenever anyone moved in the bed, the husks rubbed together and made noise."

Most of all, Andrea remembers the hunger. Due to their dire economic straits, they often had to resort to food that they found growing in the wild. Very often, his mother, and sometimes even his father, went into the fields to pick chicory. His father was especially good at finding wild asparagus. And, after it rained, the family would go up into the mountains to look for snails.

Pasta is, of course, the primary staple of the Italian diet. Andrea explains that the women would have to use bran when they ran out of flour. His grandmother would use the bran to make 'stringozzi,' long, flat noodles that resemble shoelaces. He certainly had no fond memories of this pasta, saying that *"it neither went up nor down our throats. It was like eating sandpaper!"*

But sometimes there was almost no food to eat.

"When there was nothing else to eat, a smoked fish was hung from the hook over the fire and two slices of bread were rubbed on the sides of the fish. While hanging over the fire, the fish exuded a little juice which tasted like the smoked fish on the bread. The same fish was used countless times until no taste was left. Then each of us was given a little piece of the fish."

Andrea's Parents: Antonio and Assunta
Photograph by Nicola Morano

Andrea's Move to Rome

During the Christmas holidays of 1933, Andrea was invited to stay with his father's sister Agnese and her husband Nicola in Rome because his mother had been hospitalized to treat another one of her many bouts of depression. His father accompanied the five-year-old boy to Rome.

Andrea with his father in Acuto
Photograph by Nicola Morano

"The only means of transportation to Rome was a small streetcar that ran the line from Fiuggi to Rome and took three hours, making innumerable stops on the way. During the trip I plied my father with questions about my aunt and uncle, about the city, about what I would find, about what I would have to say and about what I would have to do. I don't think that I was quiet or still in my place for more than five minutes at a time for the three seemingly endless hours of our trip."

The economic situation of Andrea's uncle, Zio Nicola, was very different from that of his father. He had a well-respected position at the Ministry of Justice and was also a professional free-lance photographer. When he arrived at their home, Andrea was completely overwhelmed by the large apartment building and by the apartment's many rooms and windows. And he was, of course, very surprised that they had indoor plumbing and electricity! There were more surprises, too.

"At dinner time I found us all seated together at the table with so many good things to eat, something that happened very seldom in Acuto. After dinner, when it was time to go to bed, I was shown my bedroom. I had a bedroom to myself, with a bed all to myself. And I was very surprised that my bed didn't make any noise. The mattress was soft and comfortable, filled with wool, which for folks in Acuto was a luxury item beyond their reach."

Andrea had arrived in Rome with only the clothes that he was wearing. In the days that followed, his aunt took him shopping to supplement his sparse wardrobe. She also bought him a toy, a small wind-up car. It was his very first store-bought toy as children in Acuto had only the playthings that they were able to make themselves from whatever they could find at hand.

**Andrea with his first toy
Photograph by Nicola Morano**

After Andrea had been in Rome for two weeks, his father returned to take him back to Acuto. But there was no way the happy boy could be convinced to leave. His departure was postponed several times until it was decided that he could live with his aunt and uncle indefinitely. As they had no children of their own, they welcomed him with open arms.

"*I had become very attached to Zio Nicola. He was very understanding and he knew what to expect from a child like me. Zia Agnese, on the other hand, although she was very fond of me, expected me to act like a mature person. She was very rigid and, for this reason, everyone called her 'The Colonel.'*"

"*Zio Nicola and Zia Agnese had temperaments that were completely opposite but they loved each other very much. They had their arguments which never, however, lasted very long. And they both considered me their son and adored me.*"

Andrea with his uncle Zio Nicola
Photograph by Agnese Morano

Although his mother was broken-hearted at giving up her oldest son, Andrea adapted immediately to his new life and did not miss his parents very much because he had not formed a strong attachment to them. In fact, he hardly knew them as they spent long days in the fields working to eke out a living or going elsewhere to find odd jobs to do. It was his grandmother Nonna Lucia who had looked after him and his numerous cousins. He describes her as a very harsh person who considered the children nuisances and left them outside most of the time to fend for themselves.

His aunt and uncle made sure, however, that he maintained contact with his family in Acuto. They often took him for visits during the school year and he stayed with his parents and siblings during his summer vacations. His sister Betta remembers that in the summer he would bring his bicycle and his scooter with him because no one in their village had them.

Mussolini's Plan for the Education of Italy's Children

When Andrea was born, the fascist curriculum had already been successfully implemented at all levels of education.

The education of youth was an important cornerstone of Mussolini's Grand Plan for Italy. American historian and social scientist Eric Johnson (2008, 62) writes that "Italy's children became special targets of the fascist government after it assumed power …

and reorganized the Italian educational system under a centralized ministry that adapted national curriculum to conform to the Fascist Party's beliefs."

Mussolini appointed Giovanni Gentile, Professor of Philosophy at the University of Rome, as his first Minister of Education in October 1922. He had the responsibility of drafting the new syllabi and the guidelines for education at the elementary, secondary, and university levels. Gentile became known as the "Philosopher of Fascism." After the fall of Mussolini in 1943, he was assassinated by anti-fascist communists in Florence.

On April 3, 1926, Mussolini created the Opera Nazionale Balilla for boys from nursery school at age 4 through the university. He banned the Boy Scouts and all other youth organizations. The name 'Balilla' was chosen to inspire the boys because it was the well-known nickname of Giovanni Battista Perasso, the local boy who, according to legend, started the revolt of 1746 against the Habsburg forces that occupied Genoa in the War of the Austrian Succession.[2]

The Opera Nazionale Balilla functioned until 1937, when it was then absorbed into the Gioventù Italiana del Littorio, a youth section of the National Fascist Party.

British historical biographer Jasper Ridley (1997) writes that the indoctrination of the youth was especially important in Italy "where every child was indoctrinated in Catholic Christianity from the very earliest age." The Balilla was created to counteract the influence of the Catholic Church. It was to instill in the boys a sense of military education and discipline and to make them aware of their Italian-ness and their future role as fascists.

P.W.L. Cox, an American professor at New York University who was interested in European secondary education, viewed these developments in Italy with alarm. In an article published in 1935, he wrote

---

[2] A statue of Balilla was erected in Portoria Square in Genoa, Italy.

> One of the most effective educational instruments that the world has ever known is the Opera Nazionale Balilla, frankly a political instrumentality created and operated to ensure the permanence and success of the Fascist revolution in Italy, with its implications of national unity, imperialism, and a strong, trained, competent people. Militarists and pacifists abroad look at this *Balilla* training with much concern. And this concern is surely justified. (Cox 1935, 267)

Cox quotes Italian Francesco Nitti, a staunch opponent of Mussolini, who describes Balilla as "a military organization directed by militia and army officers. Its members wear black shirts, learn to handle a gun, are drilled regularly, and learn the rudiments of military discipline."

As journalist Gianluca Giansanti (2016) notes, Italian children were considered, from the cradle, citizen-soldiers who were expected to serve their country until they were called to become an active part of the Armed Forces.

In author Elsa Morante's acclaimed novel *La Storia* (1974), set during the German Occupation of Rome, the central character is a school teacher who, adhering to the official syllabus, gives her students the following dictation: "The heroic Italian army has carried the glorious banner of Rome beyond the mountains and beyond the seas to fight for the greatness of the Fatherland and to defend its Empire until the final victory."[3]

The educational program also sought to instill in the children love for their leader. Posters displayed in Italian schools showed Mussolini with a happy young balilla in his arms giving him the Roman salute and the words: "The children of Italy love il Duce very much. Long live il Duce! Salute il Duce! To us!"

---

[3] English translation from *History* (2000) by William Weaver

Although Andrea should have become a Figlio della Lupa when he turned four, he was not enrolled in this obligatory educational program.

"Because my parents were very poor, as were most of the families in my village, they couldn't afford the luxury of buying me either the uniform or the toy gun. Although participation in this program was supposed to be obligatory, it was not rigorously enforced in the rural areas. So, living in a small village, I was not officially enrolled. I think that the only child in Acuto who had a uniform and was officially enrolled was the son of the mayor."

However, when he moved to Rome, the fascist capital, he was immediately enrolled as a Figlio della Lupa with the necessary uniform and weapon. Participation was rigidly enforced.

The Balilla organization consisted of several levels for students from nursery school through university.

- **Figli della Lupa (Sons of the She-Wolf)**

The youngest children were *Figli della Lupa*. This name was taken from the famous Roman legend of the she-wolf who adopted Romulus and Remus, twin boys who had been abandoned by their mother. As adults, they founded Rome on April 21, 758 B.C.

The special uniform of the Figli della Lupa consisted of the following:

- a black fez made of wool with a drawing of the she-wolf nursing the twins
- a black shirt with two white bands that crossed in the front and sketches of two heads of the she-wolf
- black leather shoes
- medium-length gray-green pants
- gray-green knee socks

In addition to the uniform, the Figli della Lupa had toy guns that were replicas of the service rifle of the Royal Italian Army. Mussolini wanted all of the boys, even the very youngest Figli della Lupa, to become familiar with weapons and to learn how to use them. Because the boys were being prepared for future military service, these weapons as well as the uniforms were an essential part of the fascist agenda.

Figli della Lupa in uniform
Photograph Courtesy of Renato Pellizzoni

- **Balilla**

When he turned eight, Andrea rose to the level of Balilla. At his induction ceremony, he swore his allegiance to Mussolini (il Duce) by reciting the following oath: "In the name of God and Italy, I swear that I will execute il Duce's orders and serve with all my strength and, if necessary, with my blood."

Andrea notes that his new Balilla uniform was very similar to the one he had worn as a Figlio della Lupa, save for two differences. He also received a new gun.

"In place of the white bands across our chests, we wore a big blue kerchief around our necks that formed a triangle on our backs

and was tied in a bow in front and held in place by a large pin with Mussolini's image on it. In place of the white belt, we wore a black band that was 15 centimeters wide and wrapped around our waist like that of a bullfighter. In place of my toy gun, I was given a real scaled-down version of the Royal Italian Army's service rifle."

**Balilla Andrea (third from left) and his schoolmates
Photograph by Nicola Morano**

In the early 1930s "Giovinezza" (Youth) became the official anthem of the Italian army and students were obliged to sing it at the beginning of each school day. After the fall of fascism, this anthem was banned.

The Italian educator and poet Vinicio Saviantoni, who also grew up in Rome under fascism as did Andrea, wrote about his experiences in his memoir (2007). Every morning, when he entered his school building, he had to give the Roman salute to an urn with ashes of WWI soldiers that was placed at the entrance. The Roman salute was adopted by the fascist regime in 1923. Some scholars doubt, however, that the ancient Romans ever used this gesture. In Mussolini's Italy it generally involved holding the arm straight out with the palm of the hand down with the fingers touching. This salute and other fascist customs were banned in Italy's post-war constitution.

The covers of the children's report cards reflected the importance of the integration of the school children into the fascist regime. Andrea saved all of his historic cards. The cover for the Year XIII of the Fascist Era can be seen below. All of his fascist report card covers can be seen in the Notes for Chapter One in the Author's Notes.

Andrea's report card for Year XIII of the Fascist Era

Mussolini wanted to bring glory to present-day Italy by attempting to recreate the great ancient Roman Empire. He chose the fasces and axe, a familiar Roman symbol, for the fascist symbol.[4] This symbol displays a bundle of grain and a hatchet attached to it.

---

[4] Many Americans might be quite surprised that this symbol was also popular in Washington, DC in the early 20th century. See Notes for Chapter One in the Author's Notes.

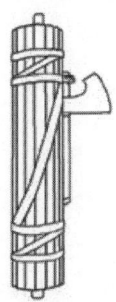

**Fasces, a bundle of wooden sticks with an
axe blade emerging from the center
Drawing by Betsy Mignani**

In ancient Rome the lictors were the bodyguards of the powerful magistrates who controlled the military and government entities. They walked behind their designated magistrate when he was in public and protected him, ready to strike with their hatchets in case he was attacked.

The fascist symbol was made into a lapel pin that men had to wear on their jacket collars. If one was anti-fascist, he probably referred to it (in private, of course) as a *cimicetta* (a little bedbug). P.N.F. stands for Partito Nazionale Fascista (National Fascist Party).

**The fascist lapel pin with party logo
Drawing by Betsy Mignani**

Fascist Saturday

On June 20, 1935, Mussolini instituted Fascist Saturday. For the children this meant that, on Saturdays, they had only half a day of school followed by special activities in the afternoon. One of the courses in the curriculum was *Fascist History and Culture* and Andrea's grade for this course was determined by his performance at these Saturday activities.

Military Maneuvers

The boys would go home for lunch and then return to their schools in the afternoon for the military maneuvers. Andrea and the other boys were very proud to participate and to wear their military uniforms. After they had answered the roll call, they were organized in military fashion and marched through the streets of their neighborhood.

Every school had its own legion and Andrea's was Legion 33. Like the army of the ancient Roman Empire, every legion was divided into centuries, every century into maniples, and every maniple into platoons. Every legion had its own musical band.

"The band of my legion was made up of two rows of imperial drums that were of the same diameter as tambourines but they were longer and had a much lower tone and provided the beat for the music and the march. They were followed by two rows of accompanying drums and several rows of trumpets."

Andrea was very enthusiastic about this band, which usually played the triumphal march from the opera *Aida* by Verdi. He was especially impressed with the mace bearer, who was the band's most envied member.

"The Mace Bearer carried a baton with a silver knob at the top and an ornamental ribbon and marched ahead of everyone, in the middle of the street, and provided the tempo for the march, by making his baton spin with great mastery and musical ability."

- **Balilla Moschettieri (or Balilla with Muskets)**

When Andrea finished elementary school and began middle school (*il ginnasio*), he became a balilla moschettiere. As musketeers, the boys were armed with small copies of Rifle 91 (1891). They were given cartridges that shot only blanks. The Italian soldiers had been given this model in World War I. The soldiers in the first years of World War II were also given this gun and, in Andrea's opinion, this was unfortunate because it was outdated and not very effective.

The uniform of the balilla moschettiere was almost the same as that of the balilla with a few differences. Instead of the black band around the waist, the boys had a leather belt with cases for the cartridges. Instead of a fez, they wore forage caps similar to those worn by the soldiers. But, when Andrea reached this level, he and his friends did not have the mountain boots.

"We should have worn hobnailed mountain boots but I became a balilla moschettiere at the end of 1939 when Italy was in the middle of the self-sufficiency program; therefore, instead of leather hobnail mountain boots, I had to be content with a pair of shoes made of fake leather with soles of pressed cardboard without hobnails that quickly fell apart as soon as it started to rain."

Because of the economic sanctions against the country for its military aggression in Africa, Italy was unable to import important natural resources that it was lacking and the government, therefore, tried to make Italians more self-sufficient by finding substitutes. Fake leather for real leather was an example.

Special Assignments for Balilla in Rome

Children living in the capital were involved in more activities than children elsewhere in Italy. Andrea's legion often had special assignments beyond the school and their immediate neighborhood. They would be given a red postcard at school that indicated the time and place of the special event.

Honor Guards

They served as honor guards in all of the special commemorative ceremonies, for example, the Founding of Rome on April 21st, the Day of the Victory of the Armed Forces on November 4th, the March on Rome on October 28th, the formation of the Fasci di Combattimento on March 23th, and the founding of the National Fascist party on November 10th. Andrea noted that there were so many ceremonies that he couldn't remember all of them!

Military Parades

"On special occasions, all of the legions of Rome and the province of Lazio were convened for a general assembly to participate in a military parade. The parade then officially passed in review. Sometimes it was Mussolini himself who passed the parade in review. The problem with these parades was that we had to arrive at the assembly location several hours in advance of the arrival of Mussolini or of the official who was going to pass us in review. This aspect of our life as balilla was certainly not pleasant."

Hitler came to Italy for a week in May of 1938. He travelled to Rome by train and was met at the station by the King and Mussolini. During his visit he watched military parades in his honor and went sightseeing. He also visited both Florence and Naples during this visit.

Saviantoni remembers his legion parading through the squares and streets of Rome to honor Hitler. They marched, he writes, holding their muskets high in the air and waving them like flags and "looking forward toward the distant goal of becoming warriors."

The renowned Italian film director Ettore Scola, in an interview with Stefano Masi (2006), shares his own memories of Hitler's visit to the capital. The parade to honor Hitler on May 3th remained his most vivid memory of the period of fascism in Rome. That day, along with his father and brother, he left home at 5 a.m. in order to secure a good location to see the reviewing stand of the dignitaries watching the parade. They took egg sandwiches with them to eat for lunch later.

They were able to get a close look at the powerful Adolf Hitler and, despite the extravagant nature of the parade and all of the hoopla, young Scola was not impressed with the man. In fact, he thought Hitler was rather ridiculous looking with his "two stupid red mustaches."

Years later, in 1977, Scola directed one of his best known films, *Una Giornata Particolare* (A Special Day), starring Sofia Loren and Marcello Mastroianni, which immortalizes this unforgettable day. This film was awarded the Golden Globe for Best Foreign Film and an Academy Award nomination in 1977 and the César Award for Best Foreign Film, the Nastro d'Argento for Best Script, and the David di Donatello for Best Director in 1978.

Sentry Duty

Saviantoni also writes about his legion acting as sentries at Palazzo Venezia, the headquarters of Mussolini, "like real soldiers." He, however, deeply regrets having lost the telegram he received from Mussolini himself, praising the boys for their impeccable service.

The Youth Games

Mussolini placed great emphasis on sports and body building. Most of the boys enjoyed this aspect of their fascist education. Andrea found it challenging as well as exciting.

"As balilla moschettieri we participated in various sports. Mussolini wanted all of us to be as fit as possible and we had to work hard!"

The boys also took part in the *Ludi Juveniles* (Youth Games). Andrea proudly participated in three of the athletic events: the 400 meter dash, the discus throw, and the javelin throw.

Cover of one of Andrea's student notebooks

Above is the cover of one of Andrea's student notebooks that highlights these games. Note the word *Vincere* (Win) on the notebook. It was a popular exhortation designed to inspire the people. Buildings often displayed these words and slogans. Many are still there today.[5]

Umberto Eco (1995, 1) writes about winning a Ludi Juveniles award.

> In 1942, at the age of 10, I received the First Provincial Award of Ludi Juveniles (a young voluntary, compulsory competition for young Italian Fascists – that is, for every young Italian). I elaborated with rhetorical skill on the subject "Should we die for the glory of Mussolini and the immortal destiny of Italy?" My answer was positive. I was a smart boy.

---

[5] See a list of common slogans in Notes for Chapter One in the Author's Notes.

Some Positive Benefits of Balilla

The children for the most part found the activities they participated in on Fascist Saturdays enjoyable. Ridley states that there were also certain positive advantages in being part of the Balilla organization.

He highlights two advantages in particular. The children had recourse if they encountered problems in the classroom. For example, if a child was mistreated by a teacher or was bullied by a fellow classmate, he could appeal to the leader of his local Balilla. Also the children who were Balilla members were given a month's summer vacation, all expenses paid. A doctor would examine each child and then recommend either a vacation in the mountains or at the seaside.

The father of Ettore Scola, however, would not permit his sons to attend these camps. Giuseppe Scola was a medical doctor and he would write medical excuses for them. He considered these ideal occasions for the spread of lice among the children. The boys were very envious of their friends because they had heard the kids were allowed to go wild in the camps.

The War Years

Andrea would never forget the fatal day in 1940 when Mussolini summoned all of the citizens of Rome, adults and children alike, to Piazza Venezia for a very important announcement.

Chapter Two

The Pact of Steel Between Mussolini and Hitler: 1940-1943

Mussolini's Declaration of War: June 10, 1940

June 10, 1940 was a critical day for the people of Italy. For several months leading up to this momentous day, Italians had been anxiously waiting to learn the fate of their country.

In 1939, after France and England had declared war against Germany for having invaded Poland, Mussolini was unsure whether or not to join them. To assist him in deciding, he asked if they would give their official recognition of Italy's conquest of Abyssinia[6] in return for his support. France was favorable but Anthony Eden, England's Foreign Minister at the time, was strongly opposed. Needless to say, Mussolini was not pleased with this response. Would he then go with Germany?

Despite Mussolini's close relationship with Hitler, it did not seem inevitable that Italy would side with Germany. Many Italians hoped that Mussolini would manage to keep Italy out of the war. Besides, most Italians did not particularly like the Germans. On the other hand, they were not fond of France and Great Britain, either. They

---

[6] Abyssinia was another name for the Ethiopian Empire that included Ethiopia and Eritrea.

did not have positive memories of their treatment by these nations at the peace table after World War I.

English historian and biographer Iris Origo, who was living with her Italian husband in Tuscany, predicts in a diary entry on April 6, 1939, that Mussolini would side with Germany. The war propaganda would present France and Great Britain as permanently blocking the way of the countries such as Italy to economic expansion. She notes that even many well-educated Italians accepted this view because they were "profoundly convinced that nothing except violence will induce the democracies to concede a re-distribution of raw materials and colonies." (Origo 2018, 31)

Mussolini, however, seemed to be seriously considering all of his options and kept the public in suspense. A photo of him piloting a plane appeared on the front page of the *Giornale d'Italia* on September 28, 1939, with the caption, "The Italian people know that they must not disturb the pilot, not continually ask for information about the route." He finally reached a decision several months later and announced that he would make his decision public.

June 10th in Rome

"The entire population of Rome was invited (actually ordered) by means of a red postcard[7] to come to Piazza Venezia to hear Il Duce make an important announcement. Of course, we all knew what his announcement was going to be."

---

[7] The red postcard was given to the children at school and mailed to adults at their homes.

Palazzo Venezia in Piazza Venezia[8]
Photograph by Betsy Mignani

Andrea went with his uncle and, because of Zio Nicola's press credentials, they were able to stand almost directly under the legendary balcony, Il Duce's favorite bully pulpit. More than 80,000 Italians packed the square and the streets leading out of it for miles.

Mussolini announced his decision to enter the war alongside Germany. He was a powerful orator and electrified the crowd. At a certain point in his speech, he barked out the following question:

Italians! What do you want? Butter or cannons?
The response from the crowd was immediate.
Cannons!

The deafening roar from the assembled multitude startled 12-year old Andrea but he was not surprised at the enthusiastic response, which remained indelibly imprinted in his memory.

---

[8] Mussolini's headquarters was located in Palazzo Venezia in Piazza Venezia, a square in the center of Rome close to the Colosseum.

June 10*th* in Acuto

While the citizens of Rome were ordered to appear in person in Piazza Venezia to hear Mussolini's fateful announcement, Italians from all over the country were commanded to gather in specific locations in their towns to hear it by radio.

Professor Mario Ticconi, the historian of Andrea's village of Acuto, describes this memorable day in his book *Acuto*. (2003, 317-321)

He writes that it was in the late afternoon on a hot summer day in the middle of harvesting season that the farm workers heard the order that they were to leave the fields and gather in Piazza Margherita for an important announcement. The assigned messenger rode around on his motorcycle, urgently blowing his trumpet and making it clear that the workers had no choice but to obey without delay.

A radio had been set up in Acuto's central piazza encircled by a row of chairs occupied by the village notables and the teachers from the elementary school. They soon heard Mussolini's voice and were not surprised to learn that Italy was going to war against the Allies.

The War Effort

The headline in the next edition of the *Corriere della Sera* read: *Italian People, Run to Arms! The Dramatic Announcement of il Duce: War against Great Britain and France.*

Thus, Italy went to war with Germany against France and England and then, after a year and a half, against the United States as well.

What tipped the scale? Why did Mussolini finally decide to side with Germany rather than with Great Britain and France?

In Andrea's opinion, the resounding victories of the German army first against Poland and then against France were one of the determining factors. He noted that this error in judgment cost Mussolini his position of power and ultimately his life.

In her diary Origo suggested another reason for Mussolini's decision: the importance of the Nazi occupation of Norway.

> After Norway – what? Every country in Europe is waiting. If the Norwegian campaign has not increased the Italians' liking for Germany, it has certainly increased their respect and fear. The cult of violence flourishes on success ... Every day brings fresh rumours, and with them the conviction that Italy too will be in before the end of the month. The real war is coming. (Origo 2018, 127)

Origo tells of a visit from an Italian army colonel who had an intense dislike of the Germans. However, she recounts,

> All the same, like every other military man, he is impressed by the brilliance and speed of the German tactics, and above all by the sheer quality and quantity of her war material – human and mechanical. Although he abhors the thought of Germany dominating Europe, he is convinced that Italy must join the war on the side of Germany. Italy has no choice. (Origo 2018, 135-36)

Andrea relates that at this point the Italians became isolated from the rest of the world. They were fed fascist propaganda and were unaware of what was happening in the rest of the world.

"The people in Rome were not even aware of what was happening in the rest of Italy."

Therefore, the climate was euphoric because the Italians heard only about the victories of the Axis powers, and young Italian fascists like Andrea felt themselves strong and invincible.

To encourage this euphoria, Mussolini, in his various speeches after the declaration of war, told the Italians that Italy had eight million soldiers ready for the various fronts of the war. They did not know and could not imagine that it was just a bluff.

In reality they were not prepared for war. Andrea explains:

"While it was true that Italy had eight million men to send to war, it was also true that it did not have the economic resources

and enough weapons to fight. I am referring to both light and heavy weapons and also to all of the logistic means and supplies that an army of this size requires."

Andrea mentions Italy's desperate need for raw materials for the war effort, in particular, iron.

"To make up for the lack of iron needed for the factories, all of the fences in Rome began to disappear. Attempts were even made to extract iron from the sands on the Tyrrhenian beaches."

Italy was already overextended in Africa. Mussolini had come to power promising to redress some of the wrongs of the Treaty of Versailles. He wanted to expand Italy's "empire" in competition with other European nations who were also seeking to expand their empires. For this reason he had invaded Abyssinia on October 2, 1935. This military campaign was dragging on, and it was a drain on Italy's economic resources and manpower.

From the very beginning of the war, the Italians began to see their deficiencies. Andrea mentions two particularly alarming examples.

The day after Mussolini's declaration of war against France and Britain, the Italian military was humiliated.

"Our soldiers were unable to cross the border into France. They were stopped by the French soldiers, who were not only inferior in number to ours but also demoralized by the enormous defeats they were suffering in the northern part of their country by the overwhelming German forces."

He also relates the initial failure of the Italian antiaircraft artillery. On one of the very first nights of the war, a small French airplane left Corsica and flew over Rome.

"Our antiaircraft artillery was set up in the Roman neighborhood of Monte Mario and, instead of hitting the airplane, it hit the terraces of several Roman apartments."

Despite all of these deficiencies, the enthusiasm for the war continued for all of 1941 and part of 1942. Even after Italy had lost eastern Africa and the United States had joined the Allies, the war propaganda was always optimistic. But many Italians soon realized that everything was not going as well as the government wanted them to believe.

The fascist government tried to cover up the desperate food shortages by trying to convince the people that certain sacrifices were not really sacrifices, that these measures were to improve their health.

Coffee, so beloved by Italians, was no longer available. Why? Because, the government informed them, it was detrimental to their health. The bad-tasting coffee substitute made from barley, caffé orzo, was much healthier. Why was meat so strictly rationed? Because vegetarianism was better. Italians were also frustrated at not being able to drive their cars. Why were private cars abolished? Because it was better for one's health to use bicycles.

However, a majority of the people began to feel the pinch of the sacrifices they were making and discontent set in. The older youth also felt the pinch and began to lose their enthusiasm for the rigorous fascist education, Andrea included.

- **Balilla Avanguardisti (Avant-garde Balilla)**

When Andrea started high school in October 1942, he automatically became an avanguardista. Up until this point, Andrea and his friends had been proud of their uniforms and weapons. They had reveled in Fascist Saturdays and the associated activities. But their attitude began to change as the war was draining the country's resources. The Balillas began to feel the pinch. The avanguardisti should have received new uniforms that were almost identical to those worn by the Italian soldiers as well as real weapons to practice with.

But, as Andrea notes,

"It was not easy to find the uniforms and those that were procured by a few fortunate ones were made of a scratchy material that emitted a smell that was not very pleasant. And the boots were completely non-existent."

Uniforms were still required for the Saturday events, but those who did not have the official uniforms (this meant most of the boys) had to make do with what they had or could find. They were not given real weapons, of course. Not even all of the soldiers in combat received weapons.

Three Avanguardisti: Silvio Riggio (center) and two other boys in 1925

But individual schools were still invited to special events, and Andrea remembers one in particular. It should have been an enjoyable outing, but it turned out to be a very frightening one for the fourteen-year-old.

"Our legion had been invited to an equestrian circus. Of course, we all attended in uniform. Several of my friends and I chose to sit in the last row, thinking that there we would be able to smoke without being seen. We young people were not allowed to smoke, especially when we were in uniform. However, we were discovered and we were sent to the commander of our legion (the Consul). He in turn called our parents to inform them of our bad conduct and he threatened to have us expelled from school. But he soon realized how scared we were and felt that we had learned our lesson. So there were fortunately no serious consequences."

- **Balilla Avanguardisti Motociclisti (Avant-guard Balilla Motorcyclists)**

When Andrea and his classmates became avanguardisti motociclisti, each boy was supposed to have his own motorcycle. But his school had only one Guzzi 500 so the boys had to take turns riding it around their school yard on Saturdays.

Andrea's school, however, was more fortunate than that of Saviantoni who writes that his school's Guzzi motorcycle was only a drawing on a gigantic piece of paper attached to a wall. There was no real motorcycle. (Saviantoni 2007, 61)

The Breaking Point: The Landing of the Allies in Sicily

The discontent increased and reached the breaking point in July 1943 when the fortunes of the Allies started to improve.

The Allies began their invasion of Sicily on the night of July 9-10, 1943. It was both an amphibious and airborne operation and ended on August 17th. The air, land, and naval forces of the Axis powers were driven from the island. The Allied merchant ships could now use the sea lanes of the Mediterranean for the first time since 1941. This was the beginning of the Italian Campaign of World War II.

As the Allies were preparing to invade the Italian mainland, Hitler diverted troops to Italy from the Eastern front, a major battleground in the war that included the Soviet Union, Eastern Europe, the Baltics, and the Balkans. Many military experts feel that withdrawing troops from this front at this time was Hitler's major tactical error.

The tide was beginning to turn against the Axis Powers in Europe. Italy's situation was about to change drastically. Mussolini's days were numbered.

Chapter Three

Civil War in Italy and The Nazi Occupation of Rome: July 1943 – June 1944

The Fall of Mussolini and Fascism

The final victory of the Axis powers no longer seemed inevitable after the United States entered the war on the side of the Allies, successfully invading Sicily on July 9th and carrying out the first aerial bombing of Rome on July 19th. When it became clear that the war was lost, Mussolini fell out of favor.

At its meeting on the evening of July 24, 1943, the Great Fascist Council (Il Grande Consiglio del Fascismo) gave a vote of no-confidence to the government of Mussolini and ordered him to resign. He agreed without protest and went to the King to hand in his resignation the following morning. The King informed him that General Pietro Badoglio would succeed him as Prime Minister. Soon after he left the meeting, Mussolini was arrested by the Carabinieri[9] and taken to a secure location, hidden from the Germans, who immediately began their search for him.

---

[9] The Carabinieri are the national gendarmerie of Italy, who primarily carry out domestic policing duties but they are also a military force and serve as the military police for the Italian Armed Forces.

The era of fascism in Italy had come to an end. Upon hearing the news, Andrea and several avanguardisti friends went to their school gym to see if their motorcycle was still parked there. No one was surprised that this symbol of Balilla pride had already disappeared. He remembers the disappointment they all felt as they reflected on the years of fascist rule and the promises that Mussolini had made to the Italian people.

"Before July 1943 we young people, who were born and raised in the illusion of the invincible and grandiose fascism, felt ourselves, all of a sudden, betrayed, undone, and demoralized. We had had enough of Mussolini, of fascism, of the war, and we had become progressively less tolerant of the lack of liberty forced on us for such a long time. To put it briefly, we had gone 'from the stars to the stables.'" [10]

A few days after the fall of Mussolini, Andrea and his friends heard about the death of their English teacher.

"Mrs. Inghilleri was my English teacher. She was young, blond, and rather attractive. She was very involved with the Fascist Party as was the principal, Mr. Landogna. When the Fascist Party ceased to exist in July of 1943, she committed suicide and Mr. Landogna disappeared."

Saviantonio was in his village outside of Rome when the news was announced on the radio of Mussolini's fall from power. He writes that all of Vallemare began to celebrate. He and his cousin Pierino ran up the stairs of the bell tower to ring the bells. His father was in Rome at the time and told his son that the streets of Rome were strewn with fascist membership cards and lapel pins. His mother, however, kept the Balilla uniform that he had loved so much. (Saviantonio 2007, 115)

But the war was not over yet. Badoglio was widely criticized for not making peace immediately with the Allies, thus giving the Germans time to take over not only Rome, particularly important to them, but also all of central and northern Italy. The American and

---

[10] Andrea uses the Italian expression "Dalle stelle alle stalle," the opposite of the expression in English, "From rags to riches."

English troops, in the meantime, were slowly and painfully fighting their way to Rome from the south.

The Signing of the Armistice between Italy and the Allies

After several months, the armistice between Italy and the Allies was finally signed and announced on September 8, 1943. The Germans were aware that their Italian ally would soon become their enemy so they were prepared for what they considered the Italians' betrayal. They quickly rounded up the Italian soldiers who had been suddenly abandoned by their own fleeing officers. (It was an immediate source of manpower for their military operations.) These Italian soldiers had even been abandoned by their King, who escaped across the Adriatic and boarded a ship headed for southern Italy so that he could seek the protection of the Anglo-American troops.

The Italians did not forgive their King for abandoning them in their hour of need. In a post-war referendum, they chose to replace the monarchy with a republican form of government. In addition, the new constitution prescribed that all male members of the royal House of Savoy must stay in permanent exile. This disposition was finally rescinded but not until October 2002, 56 years later.[11]

The German Rescue of Mussolini

Mussolini in the meantime was kept on the move as the Germans continued their search to find him. He was hidden first on Ponza and then on La Maddalena, two small islands in the Tyrrhenian Sea, and then taken to various places in northern Italy.

His pursuers finally intercepted a coded Italian radio message and discovered that he was imprisoned at a ski resort at Campo Imperatore in Italy's Gran Sasso massif high in the Apennine Mountains. It was a very difficult place to reach as it was located on a plateau about

---

[11] The Italian king's behavior was in sharp contrast to that of Norway's monarch King Haakon VII when the Nazis invaded his country. See the Notes for Chapter Three in the Author's Notes.

6300 feet above sea level. Since access from the ground was solely by funicular railway, only an assault from the air would work.

On September 12, 1943, the Germans succeeded in carrying out a dangerous glider rescue mission. They liberated Mussolini and took him to Hitler in Germany. The two hundred Carabinieri guarding Mussolini did not fire a single shot.

The Kingdom of Italy vs the Italian Social Republic

At their meeting Hitler forced Mussolini to establish a Nazi puppet state called the Italian Social Republic of Salò that stood in opposition to the Kingdom of Italy. It was located in Salò, a town on the banks of Lake Garda in northern Italy.

Not all Italians remained loyal to the central government in Rome and the King. Some of them joined the army of this Fascist Republic. Andrea suggests disparate reasons.

"Many were loyal fascists who wanted revenge after having been abruptly removed from power. They were limited in number but very aggressive and violent because they were protected by the German Gestapo and they hoped to regain the upper hand. These loyal former fascists were called Repubblichini *('Little Republicans')."*

"Some were ordinary people who lived in northern Italy and were starving. They hoped that this new Republic would give them jobs and two meals a day."

"Others were criminals taken from the prisons."

"Therefore, we suddenly found ourselves in a country divided between the Little Republicans, who were working for the Germans on one side, and the anti-fascist Italians on the other, who were fighting a bloody civil war among themselves."

Nazi Occupation of Rome: July 1943-June 1944

The Romans must have found it chilling to witness the troops of hostile German soldiers marching down Via dei Fori Imperiali from the Colosseum to Piazza Venezia. And what a sight to see German armored tanks parked in front of the Victor Emmanuel II Monument.

German tank in front of Monument to Victor Emmanuel II

The Allies had expected to reach Rome easily within a month or two but they had not anticipated the fierce German resistance.[12] The occupation of Rome, therefore, lasted for almost an entire year.

One of the longest and bloodiest battles of the war in Italy took place at Cassino, 85 miles south of Rome, where the Germans stopped the advance of the Allies. The fighting lasted from January 17th to May 18th. The loss of life was staggering with 55,000 Allied casualties and German losses estimated at around 20,000.[13]

Hardships Suffered In Rome during the Occupation

Life for the people of Rome during the German occupation was dangerous and difficult.

The Bombing of Rome

One of the horrors the Romans faced was the incessant bombing of their city, most of it carried out by the Allies. While negotiations

---

[12] This phase of the war is explained in great detail in Rick Atkinson's book *The Day of Battle: The War in Sicily and Italy, 1943-1944*.

[13] See the Notes for Chapter Three in the Author's Notes for the personal story of Olimpio Pasquale D'Onofrio whose family was severely affected by the fighting near Cassino.

had taken place between the Vatican and the Allies in an attempt to protect the city, Rome was heavily bombed and not declared an *open city* until the bombing stopped after several months.

Why did the Allies decide to bomb Rome? These bombings were in fact controversial. The fatal decision was ultimately made by Britain's Prime Minister Winston Churchill on July 16, 1943. Many questioned whether this ruthless bombing of Rome was a crime against humanity. Churchill and the British War Cabinet thought not. Their stated goal was to break the spirit of the Italian people.

The bombings killed large numbers of civilians and destroyed complete neighborhoods in Rome. For propaganda purposes, the German occupiers wanted to make it clear that this destruction was not their work but that of the Allies. They, therefore, left graffiti on buildings demolished by Allied bombs that read "Opera dei Liberatori" (Work of the Liberators).

The first aerial bombing of Rome took place on July 19, 1943, and demolished the entire working class neighborhood of San Lorenzo. Five hundred American bombers dropped 1168 tons of bombs. Three thousand Italian civilians were killed in these raids. There were few military targets in this area where the railroad station was located and a few manufacturing plants that made steel, textile products, and glass.

The destruction of San Lorenzo continues to live on today in song and in literature. Italian singer-songwriter Francesco De Gregori has immortalized this horrific day in his song "San Lorenzo,"[14] which begins with the following words:

Cadevano le bombe   The bombs fell
come neve   like snow
il diaciannove luglio   on July 19
a San Lorenzo   on San Lorenzo

---

[14] This song can be heard on YouTube at https://www.youtube.com/watch?v=e7d6EPZG5Mc

After the bombing, Pope Pius XII went to San Lorenzo to comfort the survivors. De Gregori evokes the image of the Pope, dressed in a flowing white robe, spreading his arms in prayer, looking like "an angel spreading his wings."

Pope Pius XII visits San Lorenzo after Allied bombing

Morante set her novel *La Storia* (*History*) in Rome during the Nazi Occupation and writes of the first bombing and its aftermath. The protagonist Ida and her small son were heading home to their apartment in San Lorenzo on that fateful day when they suddenly heard "an orchestrated clamor of metallic humming" moving through the sky above them. And "at that moment the air whistled, while in an enormous thunder, all the walls were already crashing down behind their backs and the ground was leaping around them, crumbled in a hail of fragments." Their apartment building was completely destroyed and everyone inside at the time was killed. The survivors, who lost everything, were forced to live in a shelter for many months. (Morante 2000, 184-85)

The bombing of Rome continued on a regular basis in 1943 and 1944, primarily by the Allies but also on a smaller scale by Axis aircraft. The statistics are appalling: 110,000 bombings, 600 aircraft lost, and 3600 air crew members killed. Before the Allies captured Rome, 60,000 tons of bombs had been dropped in 78 days. (Wikipedia, "*Bombing of Rome in World War II*")

Rome wasn't the only city that suffered Allied bombings. Livorno, Turin, Milan, and many other cities north of Rome were also heavily damaged. In all, the official count was 66,500 Italian civilians killed in the Allied bombings. The number is probably higher, however, because not all missing civilians were accounted for.

It may seem strange that Andrea never mentioned the Allied bombings that had caused so many deaths and so much destruction in Rome and elsewhere in Italy. In his article "Italy's Amnesia over War Guilt: The 'Evil Germans' Alibi," Italian historian Filippo Focardi may provide an answer. (Focardi 2015)

Focardi points out that the European nations that had suffered under Nazi occupation shaped their memory of the war based on two main beliefs: First, that their nations had struggled mightily against the Nazis and their entire population had been united against the Nazi oppressor and secondly, that the guilt for the war and its sufferings belonged exclusively to the Germans. But he goes on to say that, in each country, there were sizeable numbers of collaborators working with the Germans (one infamous example is Vidkun Quisling in Norway whose name is now synonymous with *traitor*) and that not only the Germans had committed atrocities but the victorious nations as well.

It seems that Andrea and many other Italians had been so overcome with joy and relief when the Allies arrived to liberate them that they forgot what the victors themselves had done to them during the war. They hailed the Americans in particular as heroes.

The aerial bombings were not the only the danger. A perilous situation existed on the ground. Andrea had to remain vigilant and he could never forget that Rome was under occupation. The Germans were there and they were in charge. And they considered the Italians traitors for having switched sides in the war. That was unforgivable.

Student Skirmishes

Andrea writes about the tension in front of his high school every morning.

"When we arrived, there would always be two groups of university students who were graduates of our high school – one fascist and the

other antifascist. Each group was trying to attract the high school students to its side. Almost every day skirmishes broke out between the two groups."

Round-Ups (or Military Sweeps)

The Germans were in dire need of manpower so they began to round up young Italian men. Andrea and his friends lived in constant fear of being taken away. He writes,

"It was dangerous for all of the able-bodied men because every day there was the possibility of being caught and sent to work on Germany's defense projects in Italy or in the war industry in Germany. We students had a special pass that, unfortunately, did not always guarantee our safety. In other words, if you were caught, you were sent to Germany, pass or no pass."

Andrea and his male friends greatly feared the Todt Organization, the civil and military engineering organization that was involved in many engineering projects both in Nazi Germany and in its occupied territories including Italy.

Todt first came to Italy before the armistice on September 8, 1943 in order to repair the damage caused to the railway lines and other infrastructures by the Allied bombings. After the armistice its focus was on building defense fortifications and everything that was needed for the war effort such as bridges, roads, and airports.

Workers were needed, of course, and recruitment offices were set up around the country. Italians who volunteered were offered the choice of going to Germany to work or of working in Italy. Not surprisingly, an insufficient number of Italians volunteered so the Germans resorted to the round-ups. The first round-up of men in Rome took place on September 29, 1943, and these round-ups continued throughout the Nazi occupation. (Guerrazzini 2016)

"This was the way we lived, day after day, always living with the fear of being rounded up. We were occasionally forced to spend some time in the mountains outside of Rome to escape the round-ups."

Sometimes anti-fascist Italians put themselves in harm's way unnecessarily. Andrea would occasionally become involved in situations that he could easily have avoided. He gives some examples.

A Show of Disrespect for the Fascist Flag

"One day I was walking with my friends along a street in the center of the city when a procession of Italian fascists appeared along our route. In such circumstances it was obligatory for pedestrians to stop and salute the fascist flag. We didn't feel like doing it and so we turned our backs, pretending to look in the shop windows. Unfortunately, the captain of the squad had noticed us and he began running toward us, shouting in a very threatening voice. At this point we thought it wise to run because, if we had been caught, not only would we have been tortured but also we would either have been sent to a concentration camp in Germany or have been forced to join the ranks of the Italian fascists. Fortunately, we managed to escape."

Risky Attendance at a Secret Mass

"A few days after this terrifying race to safety, I found myself involved in an episode that gives a clear idea of how divided the country was. On 23 April 1944 students from all of the schools in Rome participated in a mass in memory of the 335 victims of the Fosse Ardeatine (Ardeatine Caves Massacre) who were shot by the Germans in retaliation for the deaths of 33 of their soldiers after an attack that took place on March 23 in Via Rasella, in the center of Rome."[15]

The Germans had a policy to kill ten Italians for each German soldier killed.

---

[15] For a more detailed account of the plot to attack the German soldiers, how it took place, and the aftermath, see Frank Korn's article "Massacre in Rome – 1944."

Memorial Fosse Ardeatine Massacre

"The mass was held in secret in the Basilica of Santa Maria Maggiore. At the end of the mass we left the church in small groups so that we would not attract attention and raise suspicion. When my group was walking away from the church, a Little Republican soldier happened to be passing by. He stopped to ask us what we were doing there, why we were not in school. It turned out to be very unfortunate for him that he stopped us."

Basilica of Santa Maria Maggiore
Photograph by Betsy Mignani

"We were quite startled when we saw him approaching us and we were also very afraid. With some hesitation, we plucked up our

courage and told him that it was our business and that he should leave us alone. Some other students, who were older than we were, perhaps university students, saw what was happening and began to come closer in order to help us. When the soldier noticed them, he suddenly realized that he was alone and he felt threatened. So he began to run away in the direction of the train station. We all began to chase him. After being chased for a few blocks, he stopped and turned around with his back against the wall of a building. When he saw that he had been overtaken, he tried to pull out his pistol. Before he could do so, however, several shots were fired at him from the midst of the crowd of students. When he was hit, he fell to the ground onto the sidewalk."

"I never found out whether he survived. None of us waited to find out. We all scattered in every direction in great haste and, a few minutes later, when we were far away and out of danger, we began to hear the sirens of ambulances and police cars."

"This was the situation and we young people, for the first time in our brief existence, began to feel like actors and not spectators. We wanted to write, with our actions, that part of history that would have redeemed us after having been tricked for so many years by an illusionist, i.e. Mussolini. This experience taught me to love freedom, especially freedom of thought and of the word, and to hate every kind of oppression."

Desire for Involvement with the Partisans

"Having become anti-fascist and anti-nazi, despite the danger of being rounded up, we still wanted to do our part against the Germans and we, therefore, took risks. We tried to get involved and to take part in the action. Once a follower of the partisans that we knew asked us to go into a tunnel under Monte Mario where 'Someone' had left some weapons that had to be collected. There were guards all over the place there but we succeeded in getting into the tunnel without being discovered. Unfortunately, or I perhaps should say fortunately, we found nothing, absolutely nothing, in the tunnel. To this day I still

don't know if our friend wanted to test us, knowing that we would not find any weapons in the tunnel, or if 'Someone' had not succeeded in leaving them there."

The Shortages

Andrea writes about the shortages.

"During the occupation there were severe shortages of food, gas, electricity, running water, and means of transportation. The months from September 1943 until June 1944 were the most miserable for the people of Rome. We lacked everything. Everything that was produced ended up in the hands of the Germans."

Shortage of food

"There was a shortage of every kind of food product, beginning with pasta and bread. The daily ration of bread was 100 grams per person. The bread was made from a material that had little nutritional value, it was black, and weighed twice as much as bread normally did. Given the minimal size of the daily ration, the bread was never enough."

"Zio Nicola, because of his job in the executive office of the penal court, had a relationship with a baker who owed him a favor. The bakery was located near Piazza Navona. Almost every afternoon, I went there on foot from my house so that we could have a couple of rolls."

"It would not have made any sense to go to my parents in Acuto for food because even there things were not much better. The general headquarters of the German police of the zone was located in Acuto and everything that was produced was requisitioned, especially wheat and corn flour, milk, and meat."[16]

"In Rome Zio Agostino, the brother of my father and of Zia Agnese, worked for an agricultural producer. Almost every day he took his products to the general market. He would try to 'forget' a

---

[16] Read about the German occupation of Acuto later in this chapter.

piece of vegetable on the bottom of his cart and then on his way home, going through Prati, he left it for us."

"Zio Nicola, before the war, had taken photographs for an English newspaper. He had chosen to receive his pay in gold coins (British pounds) and he had saved them. The exchange rate then was 2000 lira per one British pound. With one British pound he was able to buy a quintale (100 kilograms) of flour on the black market. Thus, every once in a while, we were able to eat homemade pasta."

Shortage of water

"There was a shortage of water. In the apartments there was no running water. More often than not, the fountains in the street lacked water, too. When we knew that there would be a distribution of water at the fountains, long lines would form of people carrying every type of container imaginable. Sometimes we would stand in line for hours because the flow of the water was very slow. Once my container or containers were full, I then had to carry them up the stairs to the fifth floor."

Lack of gasoline

"We lacked gasoline. For the production of gas for cooking, it was necessary to burn carbon anthracite, and all of the anthracite available in Italy was destined for the locomotives of the military trains. So vegetable carbon (la carbonella) was used, and it could not always be found."

"At home we had a heater that used carbon coke. As carbon coke was a by-product of the combustion of anthracite, we could not use our heater because, as I said above, all available anthracite was taken by the Germans. Instead we used a carbon brazier that emitted dangerous fumes of carbon monoxide."

No electricity

"We had no electricity. We lighted our house with candles when we were lucky enough to find them on the black market. More frequently, we had to use little lights that used diesel oil and emitted a very black smoke that left deposits everywhere. Even in our noses."

"We lived on the fifth floor of our apartment building, and the elevator did not work during this period. We had to walk up five flights of stairs one or more times every day."

No tobacco

There was also a shortage of tobacco so smokers were deprived of cigarettes. Andrea, who unfortunately began smoking at the age of 12, writes how his longing for a cigarette almost cost him his life.

"I will never forget the day that I asked a German soldier if he had an extra cigarette for me. His only response was to take his pistol out of its holster and threaten to shoot me."

My lack of money

"I never received an allowance but I needed money. So, oh wretched me, once I took some of our flour, and I sold it to our portiere to get a few liras. And it was not the only thing I took from our house. Zia Agnese still had the sheets, towels, tablecloths, etc. from her trousseau that had never been used so I dipped into this, too, as a financial resource. They were desperate times for everyone in Rome."

Nazi Occupation of Acuto

The people of Acuto expected a period of peace after the fall of fascism but the German occupation took place there as well as in Rome. In fact, the Nazis chose Acuto for their headquarters in the province of Frosinone. They set up their command center in the village's Giannuzzi Castle. They also took over part of the school building and many houses, some entirely and others partially, as well as the stables for their mule teams and horses and, after enlarging the entrances, also for their trucks. The Nazi commander often marched through the village between two officers and instilled terror in the inhabitants who were always under surveillance. With a population of only about 2500, it was hard for anyone to escape notice. (Ticconi 2003)

According to Andrea's sister Betta, the fascists were very cruel. She gives the following example. The occupiers were in charge of the food distribution and the residents needed ration cards to obtain their share. Because their rationed food was not enough, many people sought food elsewhere. But the fascists controlled all of the movements of the people to find food and, if they caught anyone stealing or exchanging food, they seized it and dashed it to the ground, right under the eyes of the hungry individual.

Andrea's father grew a very small amount of grain and his mother would take it and furtively give it to some of the poorest families in Acuto. Therefore, she would not have much left for her own family, which was very poor itself.

The meager diet of the people at this time usually consisted of polenta, a handful of beans, and pizza made from corn. Salt was unavailable and the women tried to find ways to prepare food using sugar instead. All of the bread baked in Acuto was sent to the German army fighting at Cassino and, to cut off this food supply, Acuto became a target of the Allied bombs.

The men under the age of 50, constantly in fear of the notorious German round-ups, lived most of the time hidden in the countryside, moving in groups at night from one hut to another. If captured, they would have been sent first to Cassino, where the fighting between the Germans and the Allies was fierce, and then, if they survived, to Germany to work in the factories there for the Nazi war effort.

Looking Ahead: The Allied Victory

Rome was finally liberated by the Allies on June 4, 1944. The fighting in Italy, however, continued and most of Italy north of Rome was occupied until the end of the war in May 1945.

Chapter Four

The Liberation of Rome in June 1944 and Continued Challenges

The Arrival of the Allied Troops in Rome on June 4th

The headline in *The Stars and Stripes*, the newspaper of the U.S. military, screamed:

We're in Rome!

"Finally, after nine long months of waiting and of enormous dangers and sacrifices, we were liberated! The Allies arrived in Rome on June 4, 1944!"

"So much enthusiasm, so much euphoria, so much abundance! The American and English soldiers and others of all the races, even Japanese, threw from their trucks and their tanks, as they passed by, cigarettes, chewing gum, candy, chocolate, and cans of meat, beans, Viennese salami, Spam, and other things. After months of absolutely nothing, everything was eagerly accepted."

Americans distributing chewing gum to Italian children

"On the morning of the following day, June 5, military columns of the Americans continually passed near our house in Via Ottaviano. They were heading north, chasing the retreating Germans."

Arrival of the Allies in Acuto

Historian Mario Ticconi writes that the people of Acuto were also jubilant on June 4th as the Allies liberated their village as well. They first heard the noise of the Allied tanks arriving on the outskirts of town and then they saw the column of tanks come into full view, "advancing like a long metallic serpent" toward the center of town.

The entire population of Acuto rushed to greet the liberators and the soldiers distributed chocolate, cigarettes, sweets, cans of meat and loaves of white bread. They parked their tanks, "which seemed more like toys of peace than machines of war." A distribution center was set up with food, medicine, powdered milk, and cigarettes. The air was saturated with the intense odor of Camels and Lucky Strikes. The celebrations lasted until the wee hours of the morning.

When the Allies left the next morning, reality set in. The people of Acuto soon felt hunger again and they lacked water as the aqueduct had been damaged by the fighting. Andrea in Rome and his family in

Acuto experienced the same emotions – the great joy at their liberation from the Nazis but the desperation from continued hardships.

Several More Months of Deprivation in Rome

"The liberation of Rome did not mean that everything in Rome was instantly fine. Life did not return to normal in Rome, and the war continued in northern Italy until the Armistice was signed almost one year later."[17]

The war finally ended when the German command in Italy signed the surrender on April 29, which became effective on May 2, 1945.

Food Shortages and Andrea's Bicycle Ride to Acuto

"Food products began to arrive on the market very slowly but they were more expensive than before due to the inflation caused by the heavy spending of the Italian government for the Allied forces of occupation and by the black market."

"A few days after the liberation of Rome, I asked my friend Antonio to lend me his bicycle so that I could go to Acuto to get some food supplies. The bus was not back in service yet. Acuto was 70 kilometers from Rome and it took me six hours to get there. I didn't find very much there that I could bring back to Rome. A friend of our family, taking advantage of the situation, gave me a little bag of beans to take to his daughter in Rome. I was sorely tempted to keep the beans for myself."

"As I was returning to Rome, the brakes on the bike started to fail. In order to brake, I had to use my shoe on the back wheel, and, given the length of the trip, when I arrived at Antonio's house, the tire was completely consumed and there was no way at that time to get a replacement."

"While I was in Acuto trying to find some food, I saw my baby brother Mario for the first time. He was just a little over a month old

---

[17] Personal stories of surviving the Allied bombings in Livorno, a city north of Rome, may be found in the Notes for Chapter Four in the Author's Notes.

and was being taken care of by our neighbor Silvia Torroni. Let me explain why my mother was not taking care of him."

"A few days after Mario was born, while the German troops were retreating along the Via Prenestina that ran alongside Acuto in the Valle del Sacco, the Allied artillery was bombarding them from the valley on Via Casilina and precisely from the nearby town of Anagni. Unfortunately, some of the shells hit homes in Acuto and there were fatalities. One of these barrages hit the house above ours and caused our ceiling to cave in and fall on the bed where, just a few seconds earlier, my mother had been resting with baby Mario next to her. The shock was so great that my mother had a nervous breakdown that lasted for several months. Her condition was so serious that she could not even take care of my little five-year-old sister Lucia. So I decided to bring Lucia to Rome to live with me and our aunt and uncle. Signora Silvia took care of Mario full time for the first year of his life."

Lack of Electricity and Gasoline and Andrea's New Year's Eve Bravura

"Street lighting did not exist in Rome. The electrical grid had been completely destroyed by the Germans as well as the system for the distribution of the water and the gas."

Gasoline was one of the items most in demand at this time in Rome. Andrea tells of the theft he and a friend carried out to obtain some.

"It was New Year's Eve. It was the only time I was allowed to stay out all night to play cards or bingo at the house of a friend. While walking on the dark streets of Rome, my friends and I noticed a jeep with no one in it. My friend Antonio managed to find a pair of gloves, and I found a gas tank. So we took the gas from the jeep. I sold it and so I had the money to play cards and also to buy a bottle of spumante for our party. I am absolutely not proud of what I did, actually I am ashamed, but this was the result of all of the deprivations that we had been subjected to."

"So several months of deprivation went by but we saw the light at the end of the tunnel, thanks to the help on the part of the Allies, who sought to alleviate our pain with the plan of UNRRA[18] assistance."

Punishment of an 'Easy' Italian Woman and My Arrest

"With the Allied troops permanently in Rome and perhaps in other parts of Italy, a new social phenomenon began to take place. Many young Italian women were enticed by the possibility of making friends with an American or English soldier so that they would have access to all of 'the good things' that they wanted."

"The Italian men, especially the sailors, began to hunt down these 'easy' women. They went around in groups and, when they saw a woman in the company of an Allied soldier, they followed her. When they had a chance, they got close to her, isolated her from her companion, and shaved all the hair off her head. Unfortunately, even the women who had honest relations were caught in the middle. The police patrolled the streets to try to protect the women from this type of aggression but they could not be everywhere."

**Public humiliation: Head shaving of two Italian women
Photograph by Victor Sierra**

---

[18] The United Nations Relief and Rehabilitation Administration (UNRRA) was an organization founded in 1943 during World War II to give aid to areas liberated from the Axis powers.

"One Sunday, around noon, while I was walking with a group of friends in Via Cola di Rienzo, we heard a ruckus coming from a side street, Via Fabio Massimo. It was precisely one of these groups that had caught a woman and she was resisting. While we were there watching what was happening, a police car arrived and, since we were close by, we were caught, pushed into the car, and taken to a cell at the nearby police station."

"This police station was directly in front of the trattoria of my friend Antonio, who had been caught along with us. Antonio knew an agent at the police station and asked him to tell his father that he was being held in a cell. After a few hours Antonio was released. He notified my uncle that I was at the police station and, after a short time, Zio Nicola arrived to get me."

"But it did not go smoothly for me. As soon as he entered the cell, my uncle hurled himself at me, even before he knew what had actually taken place, and delivered a resounding slap to my face. I was luckier than my other friends, however, who had to spend the night in the cell before they were released the following morning."

Discovering Abandoned War Materials in Acuto

"I returned to Acuto again toward the end of August of that same year [1944] for a little bit of vacation. We were still at war and one knows that, when two belligerent armies are crossing a certain territory, they leave behind them a lot of destruction and also an enormous quantity of war materials."

"My friends from Acuto and I found, in Colle Burano, a deposit with a rather large quantity of weapons: projectiles for the German Cannon 88, Italian hand grenades that were designed only to frighten and not to kill, and German hand grenades that had levers and were really deadly."

"Very stupidly, we took these artillery projectiles and, banging the part with the point, we tried to loosen them up so that we could extract the sticks of combustible balestite inside. We then made torches."

"When we returned to Acuto, near Piazza S. Nicola, one of the torches fell from the terrace and landed in the woodpile of Signora Poce. The wood caught fire. Fortunately, there was someone nearby who succeeded in putting out the fire before the flames spread."

"We also practiced throwing the hand grenades in the air against the electricity wires. Evidently, we had a guardian angel that protected us and saved us from tragic consequences."

Andrea Joins the Allied Troops

Andrea had another story that he frequently shared with anyone who would listen but for some reason did not mention in his memoir.

One day he and a friend decided to join the Allied troops in the north where the war was still raging. They found a truck driver who was going north the following day and was willing to give them a lift.

The following morning Andrea sneaked out of his house early, before his aunt and uncle were awake, and arrived on time at the departure point. He and the driver waited in vain for his friend and finally had to leave without him. The trip north was long and arduous because of the need to avoid the areas where there was fighting. They finally arrived at Andrea's destination and he was able to sign up for service. After a few weeks of orientation and preliminary training, he and his unit were sent to Rome for final preparation.

After he arrived at the barracks in Rome, Andrea called his aunt and uncle to explain why he had suddenly disappeared. Zio Nicola answered the phone and told Andrea that his aunt was very ill and that he would come to get him.

When Zio Nicola arrived at the barracks, he immediately asked to talk to the commanding officer and informed him in no uncertain terms that he was taking his nephew home because he was under age (Andrea was only 17) and had had no business enlisting. Andrea's military service, therefore, came to an abrupt end.

The Narrative Ends

Andrea's war stories end here. But the impact of living under Mussolini and fascism continued to affect him for the rest of his life. As many have said, "Once you live through a war, you can never forget it." How did the experience of living through the years of fascism and World War II affect Andrea? Read Chapter Five for some answers.

Chapter Five

Lasting Effects on Andrea of Living Under Fascism

Living under fascism for the first eighteen years of his life had profound lasting effects on Andrea. I will describe some of these, based on my personal experience observing his behavior and on hearing the many stories he told whenever he had an audience.

I. PASSION FOR KNOWLEDGE ABOUT WORLD WAR II

Andrea tried to learn as much as he could about World War II. The news that was disseminated by Italy's fascist government had always been positive. The Italians were assured that the war effort was going very well and the final victory for Italy and its allies was within reach.

He wanted to learn every detail of the conflict and so he read every book he could get his hands on. He had an extensive collection of books, in both Italian and English. I often asked him, "Don't you know everything there is to know about WW II?" He always responded that there was something new in each book he read on the subject.

His favorite book by far was the Italian translation of *The Rise and Fall of the Third Reich* by William Shirer. Although a rather lengthy book, he read it over and over again. He said that there was so much to absorb in this book that one reading was not sufficient.

He was very eager to talk to people with a direct connection to the war. After moving to the U.S., he enjoyed hearing what Americans would share with him. He was particularly excited to talk to Delmont Syverson and Frederick Berg, who had both served in Italy during the war.

Del was my father's first cousin whom I had only recently discovered through my genealogical research. When his son Johnne discovered that Del had relatives in Washington, he immediately bought two tickets for him and his wife to fly out from Minnesota to meet us. The main reason Johnne acted so quickly was that he knew his father had been longing to visit the new World War II Memorial and would not be able to unless he knew someone in the area to assist him.

After Del and Dolores arrived, we invited Fred and his wife Ginnie to come to our house one afternoon. It was a happy encounter for all three men as each gained a new perspective. Andrea was able to see the war through the eyes of two American soldiers, and Del and Fred learned what it had been like for an Italian teen-ager and his family living in the war zone.

**Christine, Ginnie Berg, Del & Dolores
Syverson, Fred Berg, Andrea
Photo by Marcello Meloni**

Much to everyone's surprise, Fred and Del soon discovered that they had both served in the 91st Division of the U.S. Army, Del in the

Artillery and Fred in the Infantry. They had never met in Italy, but here they were many years later, meeting at our house! Needless to say, the conversation that afternoon was very animated indeed with the three men sharing their individual stories.

Del's Story

Del said that he had received a letter from Uncle Sam in the summer of 1942 telling him to report for duty. He was able to get a three-month extension because it was harvest time and he was needed on his family farm.

He reported for duty in New Ulm, Minnesota in October and became a private in the U.S. Army. He was in training at Camp White in Oregon from October 1942 until March 1944 and then he went to Camp Patrick Henry in Virginia.

A convoy of eight ships was formed on the Virginia coast off Norfolk and left for Europe on April 3, 1944. According to Del, it took 18 days to cross the Atlantic. It took so long because of the detours they had to take due to the presence of German submarines. They landed in Naples and then went to North Africa for about two months where they re-grouped. His division returned to Italy on June 4, 1944. They landed in Naples and went immediately to Rome.

"We liberated Rome!" Del excitedly told Andrea, who was thrilled to hear this declaration. They were eager, of course, to talk about that special day. What Del remembered the most was the wine and the kisses from the Roman women!

I recently learned that Andrea had told our neighbor Bill Apple that, on that day, he thought the American soldiers were the greatest people he had ever met and he too wanted to become an American.

Rome was liberated, but the war was not yet over. Del went into combat north of Rome. As he served in the Field Artillery, he was with the "Big Guns." He explained that the barrels were five feet long and the cartridges went anywhere from four to six miles, depending on how much powder you put in them. His specific job was to manage the motor pool.

He served in two combat battles. He missed the third and final one, however, because he had to undergo an emergency hernia operation and was hospitalized for two weeks. When he rejoined his company, the war in Europe was over. On May 12 the last of the Germans had surrendered. The American troops slowly began returning to the U.S.

He landed in Boston Harbor on September 12, 1945. He got off the ship and immediately knelt down to kiss the ground of the good old USA. He told us that one of the best things about being home was having fresh food to eat. No more dehydrated food!

Del was a sergeant when he was discharged on November 11, 1945. He took advantage of the generous G.I. bill and enrolled at the Mankato Vocational School in Minnesota. After graduation he became a full-time mechanic in charge of the truck fleet of the Rochester Bread Company, which later became Wonder Bread. His wartime experience, therefore, had trained him for his job and paid for his education to earn the necessary credentials.

Private Delmont Syverson
Photograph Courtesy of Johnne Syverson

Fred's Story

Fred was drafted immediately after finishing high school in September 1943. He was able to choose which branch of the military he preferred and he chose to join the U.S. Army. He became a private in the 361st Infantry Regiment, B Company, 91st Division and left with his division for Europe in the spring of 1944.

He too was among the American soldiers who liberated Rome and then departed immediately to chase the retreating Germans. The division was in the Arno Valley until September 9 and then headed to the North Apennines where they remained from September 10 until April 4, 1945. Their progress was extremely slow because of the strong German resistance.

Fred vividly remembers the Gothic Line, an enormous obstacle that delayed the Allies' progress up the Italian peninsula, similar to the Gustav Line south of Rome. This virtually impregnable defensive line crossed Italy from East to West along the summits of the northern part of the Apennine Mountains. According to author C. Douglas Sterner (2008), the Germans created "more than 2000 well-fortified machine gun nests, casemates, bunkers, observation posts and artillery fighting positions to repel any attempt to breach the Gothic Line."

Fred shared some of his most memorable and undoubtedly frightening memories of his duty in northern Italy.

On April 25, 1945, Fred was guarding his platoon command post near Cerea, a small town near Verona, when he observed ten enemy soldiers in front of him. Without hesitation, he opened fire and, when his ammunition was finished, he grabbed a carbine and maintained heavy fire while the enemy's bullets were sailing through the air. The enemy was completely disorganized. Two were killed, three wounded, and five were forced to surrender.

Later he detected more enemy riflemen moving toward his platoon. He immediately found a place to conceal himself and waited for them to get closer. When they were within a few yards, he started to fire, taking them by surprise.

An account of this incident was later described in a newspaper article[19] after the war and praised Fred's bravery.

> Private First Class BERG courageously held his position and maintained a constant stream of fire. After he wounded one, the remaining three were quickly captured by his comrades. His prompt, courageous action and devotion to duty reflects credit on himself and on the Armed Forces.

The Army officially recognized Fred's bravery and he was awarded the Silver Star medal, which is given for combat valor.

Fred's happiest memory of the war was the day the Germans evacuated the town of Livergnano on October 13, 1944, and the Allies moved in. He will always remember the very warm reception that the Americans received from the people of the town. It was the beginning of a friendship that has lasted now for more than 50 years, with frequent reunions taking place on both sides of the Atlantic. Many Americans including Fred were present for the opening of Livergnano's WWII Museum. Later, on one of our visits to Italy, Andrea and I had the opportunity to visit the museum and to meet some of the local people.

---

[19] Fred's wife showed me the yellowed newspaper article but there was no information as to its source or date. She thought it had been published in the *Tennessee Times*.

Fred Berg (left) with T/Sgt. Clifford Tomblin, T/4 "Doc" Mays, and Sgt. Victor Fitzpatrick, January 28, 1945, Montecatini, Italy

Photograph Courtesy of Fred and Ginnie Berg

Friendship with a Russian World War II Buff

Andrea enjoyed conversing not only with men who had fought in the war but also with other World War II buffs like himself. Another person who became a special friend of his was Ivan Olesov, who grew up in Russia and, although he was too young to participate, developed a passionate interest in the war. He and Andrea talked endlessly about the war. Andrea was very eager to learn about the war from a Russian perspective.

Andrea bequeathed his complete World War II book collection to Ivan, who bought a special bookcase to house these books. His wife Larisa then designed a plaque for it inscribed with the following words:

In Loving Memory of Our Dearest Friend Andrea Meloni
The Andrea Meloni WWII Book Library

Ivan with his wife Larisa
Photograph by the author

II. PREOCCUPATION WITH HUNGER

Andrea had suffered from hunger for so many years that he never quite got over his preoccupation with food. At first I found this quite extraordinary. Why did he still think about the days so long ago when he was hungry?

It was rather ironic that he was born into poverty and often went hungry the first five years of his life. But, when his life changed dramatically after he moved to Rome, he thought he would never be hungry again. Then came the war and the suffering returned. He found himself again suffering not only the lack of food but also the lack of electricity and water. Again!

III. LOVE OF FREEDOM AND HATRED OF EVERY KIND OF OPPRESSION

His experience taught Andrea to love freedom, especially freedom of thought and word, and to hate every kind of oppression. In fact, he could not tolerate hearing someone tell him what to do and he admitted that he felt a certain satisfaction every time that he had the opportunity to be in charge.

He wanted to be the one in our family who was the boss. This didn't go over too well with me as an American woman or with our sons who were American as well as Italian. We would chuckle sometimes when we felt he was becoming too dictatorial and I would call him "Benito." This quickly brought him back to reality! He would sometimes laugh good-naturedly but not always.

IV. DESIRE TO BE A CITIZEN OF THE WORLD

After Mussolini's fall from power, Andrea wanted to be a citizen of the world. He resented the way Mussolini had hidden the world outside of Italy from him. Actually, Mussolini hid from the Romans not only what was going on outside of Italy but also what was going on outside of Rome in the rest of the country.

Andrea wanted to learn about everything that was going on in every corner of the world. He relished meeting people from other cultures so that he could recognize their similarities and differences from himself.

My profession was a perfect fit for him. I taught academic English to students from all over the world who were enrolled in degree programs at George Washington University. He thoroughly enjoyed interacting with them and learning about their countries. And my students thought it was pretty cool that their professor was married to a foreigner! They felt a real affinity with him and were eager to talk to him, especially about his native country and his adaptation to life in the United States.

We would often host end-of-the-semester parties at our home. We would also invite several students to our home for special holidays such as Thanksgiving and Easter. Andrea was delighted to sit at the head of the dinner table surrounded by representatives from many different cultures.

V. LONGING FOR PEACE

Lastly, Andrea wanted to live in a world in peace where everyone got along. He knew there was no hope for this, but he said that he had had enough of oppression and war. He was always ready to join me at all of the anti-war protests in Washington.

Returning from a protest against the war in Iraq
Photograph by the author

Chapter Six

Andrea's Postwar Life in Italy and The United States

In his memoir Andrea wrote about his life from his birth in Acuto in 1928 until the end of the war in 1945. After the war he finished his studies and worked as an accountant in the Ministry of Public Works for 20 years. He then decided to go into business for himself because he had always wanted to be his own boss. I met him shortly after he started his successful gift box company, Scatolificio Meloni.

Let me give some background to explain how I found myself in Rome in September 1966. Unbeknownst to me, my fate had been determined exactly ten years earlier in September 1956.

I will never forget my first day of Latin class in high school. I was thrilled when I opened my textbook and read the words, "Italia paeninsula est." I was going to learn Latin! And I had a wonderful teacher, Miss Hunter, who had a passion for Roman history. I soon decided that my number one goal in life was to go to Rome. But I thought that I should learn Italian first so that I could speak to the Romans when I got there. After four years of Latin in high school, I had my chance to study Italian in college.

I went to Wells College where I majored in Italian language and literature. I then went to the University of Florence in Italy for my Master's degree in Italian. My career objective was to teach Italian at the university level. Before settling down professionally, however, I wanted to live in Rome. This had been my dream so my plan was to spend two years there, perfecting my knowledge of Italian and becoming familiar with the city.

I moved to Rome in the fall of 1966. Through an Italian friend, I had learned of a woman who rented rooms in her apartment so I readily found a place to stay. I then looked for a school where I could teach English to support myself. I found a position immediately and so my two-year plan was set.

I started teaching at the English School on Via Lucullo, located a few blocks from the American Embassy. My hours were from 9 am to 9 pm. Since I did not have kitchen privileges where I lived, my landlady told me of a nice *tavola calda* in a piazza nearby. So when I finished teaching, I would usually stop there for a light dinner before going home.

I didn't realize it but I was being watched. Someone who also ate there frequently had his eye on me. When he arrived, he would immediately ask Romano, the owner, whether I was there or not. However, he took his time before finally approaching me.

As it turned out, I had not gone to the tavola calda my landlady had intended. She had not specified which one and I had not realized that there were *two* in the piazza. I had gone to the wrong one. But, to make a long story short, I ended up marrying this very special Roman and spent fifty wonderful years with him. We agreed that I had actually been led to the *right* tavola calda by divine intervention.

Wedding in the Sala Rossa

We were married in the Sala Rossa of the Capitoline Museum in Rome. Instead of only two years in Rome, I ended up staying ten years. We then moved to the States with our two sons, Adriano and Marcello, and settled in the Washington, DC area.

Although Andrea went to live in Rome at a very young age and became very much a Roman, he always kept in close touch with his family in Acuto and felt very much at home there. Because of his warmhearted family, I felt at home there as well.

Our last visit to Acuto together – Summer 2011

Author's Notes

These notes contain references to a variety of additional materials that might be of interest to readers including personal stories, books, photographs, videos, movies, and images.

Notes for Chapter One

Photographic Tours of Acuto

Two brief photographic tours of Acuto are available on YouTube.

(1) "Acuto Nice Medieval Town near Rome" with no sound (5 ½ minutes)
https://www.youtube.com/watch?v=XbdYGvxXikk
(2) "Acuto" with background music (1 ½ minutes)
https://www.youtube.com/watch?v=fRnsezDNdAA

Video Tour of Acuto

A delightful video tour of Acuto is available on the Comune di Acuto's Facebook page.

(3) «Acuto: Incantevole borgo della Ciociaria» with commentary in Italian (12 min) https://www.piccolagrandeitalia.tv/video/acuto?fbclid=IwAR1WLcodDAJqXGAQmRXKJzUygspdTiyoZEKGjz_iZqjKYi6nVVvjjxrMwDs

Gold Coin with Lictors

The gold coin below that was found in Dacia shows a Roman magistrate followed by two lictors, his bodyguards.

Roman consul accompanied by two lictors carrying fasces

The Fascist Symbol in Washington, DC

U.S. Dime with the Fasces

The fasces symbol became popular with prominent architects for federal buildings in Washington in the 1920s and 1930s because of its association with classical architecture.

Cass Gilbert went to Italy in 1927 to get marble for the Supreme Court building. While there, he met Mussolini and was very impressed by him.

C. Paul Jennewein studied for three years at the American Academy of Rome and incorporated the fasces in his design for the Department of Justice. He also used them on the Arlington Memorial Bridge, which connects Washington to Virginia and was completed in 1932.

Roger Morigi, an artist from Italy, used the symbol on the façade of the Department of Justice building, finished in 1935.

When Adolph Weinman designed the Mercury dime, he chose the fasces as a symbol, not for fascism but for the United States: many smaller, weaker states combined to form a strong nation. (Kontorovich 2014)

Video of Balilla Moschettieri Mounting Their Guard

https://www.bing.com/videos/search?q=balilla+moschettieri&view=detail&mid=8AD789487D00D4745F668AD789487D00D4745F66&FORM=VIRE.

Films of Military Parades

Many documentary films showing these parades are available on the Internet. The following film gives an excellent view of marching children.

https://www.youtube.com/watch?v=hOEmLAfzVRg

Video of Ludi Juveniles (Youth Games)

https://www.youtube.com/watch?v=TjPoUsb8bLA

Recording of Mussolini Speaking

https://www.youtube.com/watch?v=CfS8AulsYRk

Report Card Covers from the Fascist Era

Opera Balilla
Year XIII of the Fascist Era
Academic Year 1934-35
First Grade
Ministro Educazione Nazionale (National Ministry of Education)
Symbols: Roman eagles and a fascist hatchet

Opera Balilla
Year XIV of the Fascist Era
Academic Year 1935-36
Second Grade
National Ministry of Education
Symbol: A fascist hatchet

Opera Balilla
Year XV of the Fascist Era
Academic Year 1936-37
Third Grade
National Ministry of Education
Illustration: Student soldiers with guns and cartridge belts

Gioventù Italiana del Littorio (Italian Youth of the Lictor)
P.N.F.= Partito Nazionale Fascista (National Fascist Party)
Year XVI of the Fascist Era
Academic Year 1937-38
Fourth Grade
National Ministry of Education
Symbols: Fascist hatchet
    M = Mussolini's official signature
    Slogan: Book and rifle, perfect fascist

Gioventù Italiana del Littorio
Year XVII of the Fascist Era (A. XVII E.F.)
Academic Year 1938-39
Fifth Grade
National Ministry of Education
Symbols: Fascist hatchet, Roman shield
    M. = Mussolini's official signature

Popular Slogans

Many of these slogans can still be seen on buildings in Rome.

- *Viva il Duce!* (Long live the Leader!)
- *Il Duce ha sempre ragione* (The Duce is always right)
- *Libro e moschetto – fascista perfetto* (Book and musket – perfect fascist)
- *Viva la morte* (Long live death)
- *Tutto nello Stato, niente al di fuori dello Stato, nulla contro lo Stato* (Everything in the State, nothing outside the State, nothing against the State)
- *La Guerra è per l'uomo come La maternità è donna* (War is to man as motherhood is to woman)
- *Molti nemici, Molto onore* (Many enemies. Much honor)
- *È l'aratro che traccia il solco, ma è la spada che lo difende* (The plough cuts the furrow, but the sword defends it)

Notes for Chapter Three

Personal Story: Life in Coreno on the Gustav Line

In his unpublished book *Storia Corenese 1943-1945 e della mia famiglia* (The History of Coreno 1943-1945 and of my family), Olimpio Pasquale D'Onofrio writes about the suffering of his family and of all the inhabitants of his village Coreno when it was occupied by the Germans during WWII.

He tells how September 8, 1943 had been a day of great rejoicing in Coreno. The church bells tolled and everyone rushed outside to celebrate. They had just heard that the Allies had arrived in Naples and were expected to arrive soon in Coreno. The war and their days of suffering would soon be over.

But the Germans unfortunately beat the Allies to Coreno and the suffering would become much worse for its inhabitants. Hoping to stop the Allied advance up the peninsula to Rome, Field Marshal Albert Kesselring had ordered the building of a line of fortifications across Italy from the Tyrrhenian Sea in the west through the Apennine Mountains to the Adriatic coast in the east. This line, which became known as the Gustav Line, unfortunately passed right through Coreno.

Soon after their arrival, the Germans began their infamous round-ups of able-bodied men whom they first sent to nearby Gaeta and then to Germany to work. D'Onofrio's father was able to escape the first round-up by hiding in a pile of straw. Many inhabitants fled in terror with no plans as to where they would go and what they would do. They became refugees. The D'Onofrio family eventually fled as well.

When the Allies arrived, intense fighting began along the line. Almost the entire village of Coreno was destroyed by the Allied bombings. Many people died, not only soldiers but civilians as well. The Germans treated the local people with increasing cruelty as the fighting went on. Coreno was finally liberated on May 14, 1944, nine horrific months later.

Unfortunately, after the war was over, Coreno suffered additional casualties. The farm workers continued to die as they trampled on the thousands of mines ruthlessly left behind for them by the Germans.

Stumbling Stones (Pietre d'Inciampo)

Stumbling stones (*Stolperstein* in German and *Pietre d'Inciampo* in Italian) are concrete cubes, each bearing a brass plate 10 x 10 centimeters, inscribed with the names and dates of victims of Nazi extermination or persecution. This project was the idea of the German artist Gunter Demnig to commemorate individuals at their last place of residence or work.

The most enduring memory of the Nazi occupation of Rome was the Ardeatine Massacre. Stumbling stones were made and placed for each known victim of this event. An example is the stone for Franco di Consiglio that was placed in front of his last residence.

Stumbling Stone for Victim of Ardeatine Massacre
Here lived
Franco
Di Consiglio
Born 1927
Arrested March 21, 1944
Assassinated March 24, 1944
Ardeatine Caves Massacre

According to Eliza Apperly in an online article for the BBC (2019 March 29), there are now more than 70,000 of these stones around the world in twenty different languages. They are located in more than 2,000 towns and cities in twenty-four countries. They represent the world's largest decentralized memorial.

Noteworthy World War II Movies

Berstein and Milza (1996, 48-49) write that the anti-fascist resistance and the post-war misery in Italy led to a remarkable production of films. They mention in particular the following neo-realist films: *Roma Città Aperta* (Rome Open City) and *Paisà* (Paisan) by Rossellini, *Sciuscià* (same title in English) and *Ladri di Biciclette* (Bicycle Thieves) by De Sica, *La Terre trema* (The Earth Will Tremble) by Visconti, and *Riso Amaro* (Bitter Rice) and *Non c'é pace tra gli ulivi* (No Peace under the Olive Tree) by de Santis.

Roma Città Aperta

This film made a powerful impression on Andrea. He watched it many times after it became available for home viewing. He himself had lived through this period of terror in Rome. He was particularly moved by the dramatic scene of a round-up.

In her passionate article "How the Nazi occupation of Rome has gripped Italy's cultural imagination," Virginia Baily (2015) expresses her personal reaction to seeing the film when she was studying Italian in the late 1970s:

> It was one of the most visceral, gut-wrenching cinematic experiences of my life and I have carried the images and sounds from it – the old ladies stalling the Gestapo while the resistance hero escapes across the roofs, the martial music playing as the German regiment marches down a deserted street, the tortured hero slumped in a chair, the priest in his black robes – with me ever since.

Read a review of this film at http://decentfilms.com/reviews/opencity.

The King's Choice

Many other countries in addition to Italy have produced noteworthy films about World War II, some many years after the end of the war. For example, Norway, a country that suffered five years of German occupation, produced a significant film in 2016, *The King's Choice*.

When the Nazis occupied Norway in 1940, King Haakon VII tried in vain to stay with his people. He was told in no uncertain terms that he had to leave the country and find a safe haven. He was very popular with his countrymen, who wanted him out of harm's way. He reluctantly agreed and went to England with his son Olav, the Crown Prince. From there he actively directed Norway's war effort and kept up the morale of his people. At the war's end he returned to Norway as a hero; the Norwegians knew that he had worked tirelessly on their behalf throughout his time in exile.

The film *The King's Choice* tells this story. It was one of the finalists for the Best Foreign Film at the Academy Awards in 2017.

Read my review of this film at https://www.norwegianamerican.com/film-review-the-kings-choice/.

Noteworthy Television Series

A French Village

This outstanding French production gives an in-depth view (7 seasons) of what life was like for those living in occupied France during World War II. In June 1940, the Germans occupy the fictional village of Villeneuve, near the French-Swiss border in the province of Jura. The many characters represent the various points of view on both the French and German sides. It is available on Netflix.com and MHzChoice.com.

Read a review of this series at https://www.stageandcinema.com/2019/03/14/a-french-village-7/

Noteworthy Books of Historical Fiction

The Jøssing Affair by J.L. Oakley

Historian and author Janet Oakley did extensive research, both in Norway and the United States, to write this remarkable book of historical fiction about the five-year Nazi occupation of Norway.

The setting is Nazi-occupied Norway during WWII. Tore Haugland, a Norwegian trained in England by British intelligence services, returns to Norway and creates a center of resistance in a small fishing village on the west coast and organizes the smuggling of arms and supplies from the British into Norway. Oakley has well-developed characters and a thrilling, suspenseful plot. The reader learns a great deal about how local people adapt and act in a place occupied by a ruthless army.

My articles about *The Jøssing Affair* can be found in the *Norwegian American* newspaper.

For a review of the book, go to https://www.norwegianamerican.com/?s=jossing+affair

For an interview with the author, go to https://www.norwegianamerican.com/an-interview-with-j-l-oakley/

The Moon is Down, John Steinbeck's War Propaganda Novel

During the war the well-known American writer John Steinbeck (1942) wrote a novel entitled *The Moon is Down*. It is set in an unknown country during an occupation by an unnamed country. It was widely assumed that Steinbeck was writing about Norway under the Nazis.

The National Steinbeck Center has the following statement on the homepage of its website:

> This is John Steinbeck's propaganda novel, in support of people living under Nazi occupation during World War II.
>
> The novel's role in bolstering Norwegian morale won Steinbeck a commendation, the King Haakon VII Freedom Cross. It was awarded for outstanding contributions to the Norwegian cause during World War II. This medal remained one of Steinbeck's most treasured possessions for the rest of his life.

Notes for Chapter Four

Personal Stories: Surviving the Allied Bombing of Livorno

My Italian friend Gabriella Testa Cahill grew up during World War II and she shared with me some of her wartime experiences in Livorno, a city located on the western coast of Tuscany.

Since it was one of Italy's most important ports, Livorno was heavily bombed by the Allies. During the month of June in 1943, over 500 people were killed and 57% of the city was destroyed or damaged.

Gabriella's Stories[20]

The First Bombing of Livorno

Nonnina [my grandmother] was frying a couple of eggs for my brunch and I was just about to eat when we heard a buzz, "like swarms of giant bees flying toward us." We instinctively repaired under the very wide arch of a door, and none too soon, as we realized that the bees of our fantasy were actually airplanes and the buzz had changed into a roar following the lugubrious whistle that accompanied every explosion.

---

[20] Gabriella sent me these stories via email in October 2019. The English translation is hers.

That is how we were introduced to the war and how we lived through it, always with the thought in mind that from one moment to the other we could be blown to smithereens.

Continuing Aerial Attacks

Our decision to remain in Livorno wasn't one taken lightly; we knew the risks ahead of us, but we were lucky because rather than living in the grip of fear, we took the bombing in stride, often quietly chuckling at some frightened people's reactions, not realizing that perhaps the reason for our snickering was our frayed nerves.

So, we remained in our home while the aerial attacks went on, leaving an unexploded bomb a few yards from our house, an outside wall badly cracked and a wake of destruction and death all around us. I still can't believe that Nonnina and I came out of it alive and unharmed.

The Bombing of the Train Station in Pisa

Another close call came on the day I was returning from Pisa where I had gone to check the results of my exams at the university. If Livorno was a choice target because of its mercantile harbor, Pisa was just as important because it was a critical railroad center, and it is there that I was caught, right in one of the underpasses of the train station.

As usual, the sirens gave the alarm and this time, in a matter of seconds, the American *fortezze volanti*, the "flying fortresses," were above us. The station was pulverized and so were dozens of unlucky people whose bodies were splattered all over the ground and against the wall.

Strange how at the moment, instead of reacting with terror at the sight of that apocalyptic scene, I looked at it with a detachment that I can only explain by saying that I was concentrating on only one thing: how to get back home. After meandering through that mayhem of rubble and blood, I finally reached a point where the street was passable, and by sheer luck, I hitched a ride on a German truck that took me within walking distance of my house.

Even stranger is the fact that I came out of that mess without a scratch, the only casualty being my pretty black suede sandals which in time of war, when leather for civilian use had disappeared, were worth their weight in gold. Of all the days, I had chosen that particular day to wear them!

Becoming Refugees

Despite the bombings, we decided to stay as long as we could in Livorno while many others left town to find refuge in the countryside. Soon after the liberation of Rome, however, the Italian government ordered the residents to evacuate the city because the frontline was almost at our doorstep. At that point, we became refugees.

We had to leave all of our possessions behind and pitch tent, so to speak, in quarters designated by the government in various localities inland. We found it very strange to sleep with dozens of unknown people in a huge space that looked more like a barn than a bedroom. Indeed, we wished there had been cows rather than all that humanity around us!

Gabriella with Italian flag
Photograph by the author

References

Apperly, Eliza. (2019, March 29). "The Holocaust Memorial of 70,000 Stones." BBC Online at http://www.bbc.com/travel/story/20190328-the-holocaust-memorial-of-70000-stones.

Atkinson, Rick. 2013. *The Day of Battle: The War in Sicily and Italy, 1943-1944*. Waterville, Maine: Thorndike Press.

Bailey, Virginia. 2015. "How the Nazi occupation of Rome has gripped Italy's cultural imagination." *The Guardian,* July 25, 2015. https://www.theguardian.com/books/2015/jul/25/liberation-of-rome-italian-imagination.

Berstein, Serge and Pierre Milza. 1996. *Histoire du XX siecle: Le monde entre guerre et paix 1945-1973. Tome* 2. Paris: Hatier.

Cox, P.W.L. 1935. "Opera Nazionale Balilla: An Aspect of Italian Education." *Senior High School Clearing House* 9, no. 5 (January): 267-270.
https://www. Jstor.org/stable/30176386.

De Gregori, Francesco. "San Lorenzo." https://www.youtube.com/watch?v=e7d6EPZG5Mc.

DecentFilms.com. *Roma Città Aperta* [Open City] (1945). Review. http://decentfilms.com/reviews/opencity.

Eco, Umberto. 1995. "Ur-Fascism." *The New York Review of Books.* June 22, 1995.
http://www.nybooks.com/articles/1995/06/22/ur-fascism.

Focardi, Filippo. 2015. "Italy's Amnesia over War Guilt: The 'Evil Germans' Alibi." *Mediterranean Quarterly* 25:4.

Follo, Valentina. "The Power of Images in the Age of Mussolini." Dissertation. University of Pennsylvania Scholarly Commons. January 1, 2015. http://repository.upenn.edu/edissertations/858.

A French Village. 2015. DVD. Available from MHz Choice (mhzchoice.com) and Netflix (Netflix.com).

Giansanti, Gianluca. 2016. "La politica pedagogica fascista: L'Opera Nazionale Balilla e la Gioventù Italiana del Littorio." *Il Pensiero Storico: Rivista Italiana di Storia delle Idee*, n. 2, Nov 2016. http://www.ilpensierostorico.com/2016/11/0-7-la-politicapedagogica-fascista-lopera-nazionale-balilla-e-la-gioventu-italiana-dellittorio/>.

GovMint.COM. *"A Fascist U.S. Dime?"* 2016. https://www.govmint.com/coin-authority/post/a-fascist-u-s-dime. Posted April 14, 2016.

Guerrazzini, Amadeo Osti. 2016. "The Todt in Italy." In *The Organisation of Forced Labour in Italy (1943-1945).* http://lavoroforzato.topografiaperlastoria.org/temi.html?id=6&cap=25&l=en.

The King's Choice. 2017. DVD. Directed by Erik Poppe. (Available from Netflix.com).

Kontorovich, Eugene. Spring 2014. "When Fasces Aren't Fascist: The strange history of America's federal buildings." *City Journal.*

Korn, Frank J. 2014. "Massacre in Rome – 1944." *The Italian Tribune*, March 27, 2014. http://italiantribune.com/massacre-in-Rome-1944/.

Johnson, Eric J. 2008. "Under Ideological Fire: Illustrated Wartime Propaganda for Children." In *Under fire: Childhood in the shadow of war,* edited by Andrea Immel and Elizabeth Goodenough et al, pp. 59-76. Detroit: Wayne State University Press.

Masi, Stefano. 2006. "Ettore Scola." In *I Grandi Registi del Cinema.* Roma: Gremese.

Morante, Elsa. 1974. *La Storia: Romanza.* Torino: Giulio Einaudi

Morante, Elsa. 2000. *History: A Novel.* Translated by William Weaver. South Royalton, Vermont: Steerforth Press.

National John Steinbeck Center. "The Moon is Down" Website Homepage at https://www.steinbeck.org/his-work/the-moon-is-down/.

Oakley, J.L. 2016. *The Jøssing Affair*. Fairchance Press.
Oeltjenbruns, Kelly. (2014, March). "The Road to Fascism: Mussolini's Transition from Socialism to Nationalism." Paper presented at the Cornell College Student Symposium, Cornell College, Mount Vernon, Iowa.
Origo, Iris. 2018. *A Chill in the Air: An Italian War Diary, 1939-1940*. New York: New York Review Books Classics.
Origo, Iris. 1984. *War in Val D'Orcia: 1943-1944. A Diary by Iris Origo*. Boston: David R. Godine.
Ridley, Jasper. 1997. *Mussolini: A Biography*. New York: St. Martin's Press.
Roma Città Aperta. 1945. DVD. Directed by Roberto Rossellini. Rome: Minerva.
Saviantoni, Vinicio. 2007. *Tedeschi a Vallemare e altre memorie*. Cosenza: Luigi Pellegrini.
Squires, Nick. 2015. "Fendi unveils restored Mussolini building as its headquarters in Rome." The Telegraph. October 17, 2015. https://www.telegraph.co.uk/news/worldnews/europe/italy/11938018/Fendi-unveils-restored-Mussolini-building-as-its-headquarters-in-Rome.html.
Sterner, C. Douglas. "Go for Broke: The Nisei Warriors of World War II Who Conquered Germany, Japan, and American Bigotry." *American Legacy*, 2008.
Steinbeck, John. 1942. *The Moon is Down*. New York: Viking Press.
Ticconi, Mario. 2003. *Acuto*. Roma: Micro Services snc servizi editoriali di Roberto Salomone & C.
Un Giorno Speciale. 2012. DVD. Directed by Ettore Scola. Rome: RAI Cinema.
Willey, David. 2002. "Mussolini's 'march' on Rome 80 years on." BBC News World Edition, March 29, 2002. http://news.bbc.co.uk/2/hi/europe/2371229.stm.

ADDITIONAL BIBLIOGRAPHY

Albright, Madeleine with Bob Woodward. 2018. *Fascism: A Warning.* New York: HarperCollins.

Atkinson, Rick. 2013. *The Guns at Last Light: The War in Western Europe, 1944-45.* New York City: Henry Holt and Co, 2013.

Baldoli, Claudia. "L'Italia meridionale sotto le bombe, 1940-44." *Meridiana,* 82 (2015): 37-57.

Ben-Ghiat, Ruth. 2017. «Why Are So Many Fascist Monuments Still Standing In Italy.» In *The New Yorker.* October 5, 2017. https://www.newyorker.com/culture/culture-desk/why-are-so-many-fascist-monuments-still-standing-in-italy

Berstein, Serge and Pierre Milza. 1996. *Histoire du XX siecle: La fin du monde européen 1900-1945. Tome* 1. Paris: Hatier.

Bertellini, Giorgio. 2019. "When Americans loved Benito Mussolini – and what it tells us about Donald Trump's rise: The appeal of celebrity authority in tumultuous times." *Washington Post,* Feb. 2, 2019.

Darkest Hour. DVD. Directed by Joe Wright. Universal Pictures Home Entertainment, University City, California, 2018.

Elkann, Alain, and Alberto Moravia. 2014. *Vita di Moravia.* Milan: Bompiani.

Haycock, Dean A. 2019. *Tyrannical Minds: Psychological Profiling, Narcissism, and Dictatorship.* New York: Pegasus Books.

Hibbert, Christopher. *Il Duce: The Life of Benito Mussolini.* Boston: Little, Brown and Company, 1962.

History.com. "America Bombs Rome." https://www.history.com/this-day-in-history/america-bombs-rome (accessed October 16, 2019).

Holmes, Richard. 2004. "Battlefields." *BBC History of World War II.* DVD. London, BBC.

Kjeldsen, Kirk. 2017. *Land of Hidden Fires.* grenzlandpress.com.

McMahon, Barbara. 2006. "Memorial unveiled in honour of allies who liberated Rome." *The Guardian.* Jun 4, 2006. http://theguardian.com/world/2006/jun/05/Italy.secondworldwar.

Moskop, Roy Lorenz. "On the Way! The Story of the 91st Division Artillery" (1947). World War Regimental Histories. 28. http://digicom.bpl.lib.me.us/ww_reg_his/28.

Pearson, Robert. 2018. "The King's Defiance." *Viking,* September 2018.

Powell, Jim. 2012. "The Economic Leadership Secrets of Benito Mussolini." *Forbes,* February 28, 2012. https://www.forbes.com/sites/jimpowell/2012/02/22/the-economic-leadership-secrets-of-benito-mussolini/#6e9a174068e6.

Riccio, Ralph. 2015. "March of the Balilla: Italy's Blank-Firing Carbine." *Military Surplus Magazine.* October 14. Tactical-life.com/firearms/march-of-the-balilla-italys-blank-firingcarbine/

Romagnoli, Nicola. 2016. Exploring the Caffeinated Legacy of Italian Fascism. December 12, 2016. https://medium.com/@Nicola.Romagnoli/exploring-the-caffeinated-legacy-of-italian-fascism-aff8b3db36.

Steves, Rick. *The Story of Fascism in Europe.* PBS TV Special. https://www.ricksteves.com/watch-read-listen/video/tv-show/fascism.

Stewart, William Kilborne. 1928. "The Mentors of Mussolini." *American Political Science Review* Vol. 22, Issue 4, November. 1928, pp. 848-869. Published online by Cambridge University Press: https://doi.org/10.2307/1945351

Tuck, Lily. 2008. *Woman of Rome: A Life of Elsa Morante.* New York: HarperCollins.

Vold, Jan Erik, ed. 2009. *Ruth Maier's Diary: A Young Girl's Life under Nazism.* Translated by Jamie Bulloch. London: Harvill Secker.

Weiss, John. 1996. *Ideology of Death: Why the Holocaust Happened in Germany.* Chicago: Ivan R. Dee, Inc.